Pelican Books
Mind Specials

Parents and Mentally Handicapped Children

Charles Hannam

Charles Hannam has three children: David, Simon and Toby.
David, the oldest, is a mongol. He and Pamela his wife live
with the problem of mentally handicapped children in their
own family. He is also interested in education: he has taught
in secondary schools and is now a Senior Lecturer in
Education at the University of Bristol School of Education.
With Pat Smyth and Norman Stephenson he is the author
of *Young Teachers and Reluctant Learners*, also published
by Penguin Education.

MIND (National Association for Mental Health) is a charity
concerned with the needs of the mentally ill and handicapped,
and with the promotion of mental health. It draws attention
to inadequacies in the health service and campaigns for better
standards of care. It runs homes, schools and hostels as well
as advisory services, courses, conferences and a public
information department. It has over one hundred active local
groups who are concerned with alleviating mental stress in the
community.

MIND, 22 Harley Street, London W1N 2ED. Tel: 01 637 0741.

D1331922

PARENTS AND MENTALLY HANDICAPPED CHILDREN

CHARLES HANNAM

Penguin Books
in association with MIND

Penguin Books Ltd,
Harmondsworth, Middlesex, England
Penguin Books Inc, 7110 Ambassador Road,
Baltimore, Md 21207, USA
Penguin Books Australia Ltd,
Ringwood, Victoria, Australia
Penguin Books Canada Ltd,
41 Steelcase Road West,
Markham, Ontario, Canada
Penguin Books (N.Z.) Ltd,
182—190 Wairau Road, Auckland 10,
New Zealand

First Published 1975
Copyright © Charles Hannam, 1974

Made and printed in Great Britain by
Compton Printing Ltd, Aylesbury

Set in IBM Univers by Herts Typesetting Services Ltd, Hertford

Contents

Acknowledgements

I am very grateful to the parents who allowed me to come to their homes and who gave me time for an interview. All names have been changed or omitted and home and family circumstances have been altered to avoid identification. All parents received a transcript of their interview and agreed to its publication.

In writing this book I have made selections, and the responsibility for them as well as for their interpretation is entirely mine. I would also like to stress that several of the experiences described took place over a wide geographical area and this is not the description of what happened in only one town or in one local authority.

I would like to thank Dr H. Temple Phillips who helped me to find some of the parents to interview. Miss M. McNaught saw the manuscript and made encouraging comments. Alison Wertheimer from MIND (National Association for Mental Health) and Jonathan Croall from Penguin Education have been really helpful editors. Mrs P. White from the University of Bristol transcribed most of the tape-recorded interviews and I was also helped by Miss S. Dyke. The Bristol University School of Education gave me a grant of money to finance the project. Ann Low Beer, Leela Grant, Pat Smyth and Norman Stephenson helped me with the final draft. But my greatest debt of gratitude is to Pamela Hannam who has helped and encouraged me all the way.

Training centres

Reference is made in this book to training centres. This was their correct title at the time of the interviews but they are now known as special schools since responsibility for running them passed to the Department of Education and Science in Spring, 1971.

Introduction

Seven families (twelve people) took part in the interviews, which took place in their homes and were recorded and transcribed later. These transcripts are the basic material for this book. Each interview lasted for about an hour and with two exceptions this was the only time I met the families and the only time we discussed the problem of having a mentally handicapped child.

Four of the families volunteered to be interviewed as the result of an appeal for 'volunteers' through the training centre and the other three families were contacted as a result of the help given by one of the parents who runs a voluntary playgroup for mentally handicapped children.

In the first instance an approach was made to a very restricted group of parents: those with a mongol child aged between seven and eight and who had a child at the same training centre that my son attended. My assumption was that parents who had the same problem as I would be ready to meet me and we would work together on the basis that we were both facing similar situations. As only three parents out of a possible sample of seventeen were prepared to be interviewed it is clear that my initial assumptions were wrong. I do not find it easy to explain this reluctance to be interviewed: of course one does not wish to reactivate painful memories, nor is it easy to talk to a comparative stranger about one's personal life — and to have what one says tape-recorded to boot!

The three families who allowed me to talk to them as a result of the appeal were middle-class and each, in their own way, had coped with their problems rather well — perhaps it is easier to talk about difficulties of the past rather than those facing one immediately. One family who had, in the first instance, agreed to meet me, wrote wishing me luck with the project and then added that they thought that it could not possibly do any good and would prefer not to be interviewed. A family whom I contacted through friends agreed to be interviewed, then felt they could not face an outsider and agreed to answer questions into a tape-recorder without me being present; then I heard that the wife lost her voice when she tried to talk into the machine. In that situation I felt that no good would come if I continued to press for help when it could only be achieved at such personal pain.

It would seem that, for some at least, talking about their mentally handicapped child is difficult, particularly when the child is still very young. The volunteers I recorded had already in their own way come to terms with the problems but, even there, I found on several occasions that the interview began with a denial of difficulties; the parents put on their public face, as it were, and only as the interview went on were deeper feelings allowed to emerge. It was almost as if a second interview began when the tape-recorder was switched off! This is a phenomenon well known to all interviewers: one almost wished one had a second tape-recorder that could be switched on when the first went off and that the less controlled and unrehearsed parts of the interview could be preserved. One husband of a family that was coping particularly well said, at the end of our interview, that when he had news that the child was mentally handicapped he had broken down and wept like a child, although he thought himself to be 'usually the hard one in the family'. Again while the interview contained the official version it was often the case that the emotional bits and grievances came out afterwards. Most people were a bit guarded about these feelings and this seems to me entirely understandable; why should they open up to an outsider? Though all assurances of anonymity were given and each family received a transcript of the interview, at the actual time it was felt better to be cautious and guarded. This is not to suggest that there is a vast subterranean area of grievance, but to say that, if there were ever a deeper or more extended inquiry in this field, more than one interview would be advisable.

People answer differently to those whom they consider 'authority' or 'them' than they do to a detached outsider. As the approach I had made to one group had come through the training centre they may have identified me with 'authority' and were therefore reluctant to come forward and express deeper feelings or even to be interviewed at all. It was certainly noticeable that the group I interviewed as the result of the playgroup contact displayed more feelings of grievance and resentment. The sample is small, the class bias is strongly middle-class and I would therefore hesitate to be dogmatic about the evidence I have collected. However limited the scope of this inquiry may be, it should be realized that those who talked to me are deeply involved and what they have to say should be heard.

The families

All names have been changed and I have also occasionally changed other details to make identification impossible.

Mr and Mrs Davis

They have one daughter at university and their mentally handicapped child, Christopher, is a mongol and is blind in one eye. Mr Davis is a successful businessman and they live in a very comfortable house.

Mr and Mrs Hopkins

They have three children. The eldest, John (eight-and-a-half), is a mongol and the other two were aged six and four at the time of the interview. Mr Hopkins is a teacher and Mrs Hopkins was a senior civil servant before she married. The family lives in a large Victorian house.

Mr and Mrs Jenkins

They have three children. The middle one is the mongol (aged seven), although rather more capable than the handicapped children described elsewhere in this book. He has an older sister and a new baby had just been born at the time of the interview. Mr Jenkins has a managerial position and they live in a bungalow on the outskirts of a large town.

Mr and Mrs Mercer

Their son, Philip, is a mongol and is the youngest of six children. The oldest of the children was taking his A levels. Mr Mercer works in the engineering industry and the family lives in a pleasant suburb.

Mr and Mrs Peters

At the time of the interview Mr Peters, a skilled craftsman, was out of work because of an accident and his wife had just broken her arm. They have two children and the second one, Mary (five), has a brain injury. The family lives in a council house.

Mr and Mrs Richards

Mr Richards was in hospital with a 'mental breakdown' at the time of the interview. They have five children, the youngest of whom (aged five) has a brain injury. An older daughter, aged sixteen, who works in a store, was present at the interview. The family lives in a council house.

Mr and Mrs Shepherd

They have two children and the second one, Stephen (seven), is a mongol. The older child, Joyce (nine), goes to junior school. Mr Shepherd is an accountant and the family lives in a bungalow outside town.

Mr and Mrs Williams

They have three children: Glynn is nine-and-a-half, Bobby eight, and Harold three-and-a-half. Bobby is possibly autistic. They live in a council house and at the time of the interview Mr Williams was unemployed.

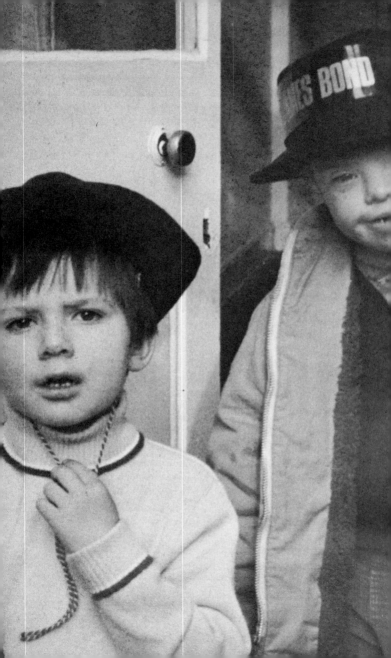

CHAPTER 1
A PERSONAL STORY

I was told within minutes of the birth of my first child that he was a mongol. The young doctor made a genuine and honest attempt to deal with the problem; what he actually said was 'I can tell you because you are intelligent'; it must have seemed to him that intelligence is good protection in the case of news of a disaster. But what **should** the poor man have said? I can't find a good formula even ten years later. I suppose that bad news is bound to be a shock even if it is broken tactfully and gently; when I was told I rushed to the library and looked for some guidance. The symptoms were all shown, but I was not reassured by pictures of hanging tongues furrowed the wrong way across, strange slit eyes, hanging bellies to illustrate a lack of muscular tone, and cross-sections of brain cells. I wanted to pour out my fears and apprehensions and I wanted to know too much at the same time. The symptoms were all outlined clearly enough; what was lacking was any information of what it would be like for me and my wife. What did we have to face, and who would help us? Could we take the strain? Why had it happened, and to us? Was there possibly a cure?

I remember a kind of roar in my head, a hot, flushed feeling reminiscent of when I was a child and had done something terribly wrong. I became very active, I saw good friends, I phoned around, but I can no longer remember what any of them said, although they were all most understanding people. They tried to give me advice and comfort, but I found it difficult to listen to them because I was in a state of heightened apprehension and could not cope with all the facts for some time. Even if I had been told adequately what was in store for me I still would not have found the information useful. All I knew was that there had been a disaster. Gradually I sorted things out: there was no cure, the disaster did not imply that we had done anything immoral, there was not necessarily any abnormality in us, there was no blame in the moralistic or biblical sense.

It was a great help to me to know that nothing we had done or not done could possibly have made any difference. The feeling of guilt was at first almost unbearable. I felt an almost Old Testament sense of having somehow done wrong and that this was a punishment. We had married when we were more than thirty-five years old, we had wanted to have a child, so there was no question of having made a 'mistake' and then pretending that it was all intentional. It seemed to me that in that case we 'deserved' a perfect child and if it was not, there must be a reason for it. I am an ambitious person, more competitive than I care to admit, and I value my own successes however moderate they seem to outsiders. Having a mentally handicapped child made me feel that I had failed. Somehow the earliest bits of morality welled up: I should have tried harder, this was not good enough. A friend arranged that I should see a psychiatrist and I talked to him before I tried to tell my wife that the child was abnormal. At that time I must have projected some of my fears on to my wife. Perhaps when I asked 'Will it drive her to breaking point?' I was really asking 'Have I reached my breaking point?' The psychiatrist was calm and sympathetic and I regained enough control to listen. I heard that the child would make progress, however slow it might be. The child would have a personality and would be educable in a limited sort of way.

Most important for me was that at last I could express my feelings of guilt, resentment and disappointment. Increasingly I thought that I must kill this child. This seemed to be a simple solution and all our troubles would be over. I was quite cool about this at first; I had to be alone with him and then I could do it. Before I went to see my wife that evening, I asked to see him and the sister wheeled him to me in his cot. I could see the signs of mongolism clearly, the shape of his eyes, the tongue that was hanging out. I had been present at his birth — a tremendous experience — and, without knowing it then, I had diagnosed his mongolism. I remember going over to him and seeing a tube in his mouth to drain away the saliva. When his nurse took the tube out, his tongue was hanging out, and I called out to my wife 'Look, he is sticking his tongue out already'. I was terribly elated and excited at that time. We had done it, a boy, immortality had been achieved! I thought him rather ugly but then I had never seen a newly-born baby before and they are supposed to be ugly. Now I wanted to kill him and it was a very frightening thing even to think about. Here was I devoting my life to the problems of educating children of all abilities, having campaigned for the abolition of the death penalty in the past, and the moment my own child did not come up to my expectations I was ready to reject him and even prepared to consider killing him. I believe that these feelings of ambivalence are entirely natural but they are nevertheless frightening and it is perhaps better to express them than have them increasing the mounting feelings of guilt and inadequacy. When I expressed these feelings to the psychiatrist he asked me whether we had given him a name. When I told him we had chosen David he said 'You may be able to throw "it" out of the window, but you can't do that with someone who is already a person with a name.' I remember feeling relieved and more secure after that interview: I had been able to listen to what had been said.

Later in the evening I was able to tell my wife and this was the greatest relief. She realized that something was terribly wrong with the child but for some time did not completely absorb what had happened. At the time when I told her about the child she had a new perfume on and was happy and radiant, having coped with the birth and having produced a child that she had really wanted to have. Neither of us can bear that perfume any more. If I smell it anywhere I am immediately reminded of that time. After leaving the hospital our friends rallied round, visited us and let us talk endlessly, but did not tell us what we ought to do. Sympathy by itself is useless. It is good to know that others feel for you, but it took me no further with my own need to deal with the shock. We made jokes to each other. It happened at Christmas and we made frivolous collage Christmas cards and sent them to all our friends. I remember being greatly amused that the only film on at the local cinema that week was 'The Mongols'. We needed a chance to express our outrage and resentment at the disaster and when we felt like that it was not much use pretending that everything was going to be easy and lovely. Some of the comfort we had offered to us is still good for a laugh: 'He will never grow up and leave you', the implication being that other 'nasty' children will persist in growing up and being people in their own right! Another crumb of comfort that was offered: 'Well, you didn't want your child to be a genius like Einstein, did you?' Equally unhelpful was the advice 'You must remove the child from the family because the other children will imitate him and become abnormal'. That one came from a colleague, a highly educated and intelligent man; but these qualities do not guarantee sensitivity and I was really worried until the thought struck me that, after all, children do not become like the family pet cat either.

Any disaster that strikes will leave one exposed to the aggressive sympathy of the 'do-gooder'. The sort of people I have in mind here are those who come 'offering sympathy', probably in a similar way to those who drive their families to the scene of a crash. Another approach we experienced was 'What does it feel like to have a mentally handicapped child?' to which we longed to reply 'We laughed all the way from the hospital'. Again there were those with strong religious convictions who came to help us with expressions of sympathy and spiritual comfort. To us they seemed to ooze patronizing self-indulgence. In other words, we were not easy people to help or support. Outwardly I put on what I hoped was a brave expression, wanting to show how well I was coping. Inwardly I was howling with rage and aggression.

Afterwards, in our own way, we had come to accept that David was going to be a mongol but there was still the problem of telling others — particularly the family. We decided to wait until there had been cell chromosome tests, when there would be absolute certainty. We really knew it was true, but we needed that sort of deadline. We reassured each other by saying, 'He does not really look like a mongol yet, let's take him up to mother's before it is obvious'. So we made our ceremonial visit with the new baby. Looking at photographs I took at the time it was quite obvious that he was a mongol and certainly not normal, but we all pretended as if nothing was the matter. I waited until his tongue was in his mouth or until he opened his eyes wide before I took a picture and those were the ones that went to the family in the United States. It took us quite a long time to say to anyone 'We had a child and he is a mongol'. It was particularly difficult to be polite to cheerful inquiries as to how the new baby was and to explain not only that he was well, but that he was abnormal. I talked to a teacher from a school for educationally subnormal children. 'What were mongols like to teach?' He said 'Oh, you mean the ones with their tongues hanging out; no bloody use at all; we had one once but he was just a nuisance, kept on sticking his fingers into electric plug holes, had to get rid of him; they go to special schools usually, anyhow why are you so interested?' I was not able to tell him why and kept the conversation on an academic level.

The memory of David's early years are still something of a nightmare to me. Of course part of the difficulty was that we started having a family rather late and some of the things I found hard to tolerate have really been due more to the fact that I had a child to live with and to adjust to, rather than David's abnormality. In fact the first months were so normal that we began to have irrational hopes that the doctors might have been wrong or that we represented the exception to the rule. It was certainly not all misery and hell during the first twelve months or so; I can remember the delight I felt when he smiled and when he sat up for the first time. To encourage his powers of observation I fixed a mobile over his cot, we talked to him a lot and tried to stimulate him, and occasionally there were encouraging responses. I want to underline the fact that he is able to make progress, because when he was born I suspected this to be out of the question. As David was our first child we had very little idea of what was meant by 'normal' progress and we accepted the slowing up that came after the first year without undue distress, because we simply did not know what we were missing.

Having the next child was an important decision and we decided to go ahead after we had talked to a geneticist. Despite reassurances and the knowledge 'that lightning never strikes twice in the same place' (but statistically there is no reason why it should not!), waiting for the second child to be born was very disturbing and I found myself rehearsing comforting speeches to my wife in case everything should go wrong again. I was planning to kill the child if he turned out to be abnormal and had quite elaborate fantasies on how I would set about it. Much later I admitted this to my wife, and we found we had been rehearsing for possible disaster at the same time. She had similar fears, but we had not been able to admit these to each other. I was sleeping badly and tried to forget about the problem by working hard and investing more and more energy in it. It must have been infinitely harder for my wife. For me there was an abnormal child only when I came home in the evening and as time went on the stabbing realization of disappointment and resentment became less, but I still wonder what it must have been like to be with the 'failure' continuously. I can hardly describe the relief when the second child was found to be normal. I was there at the birth, and, the moment I saw his crumpled face with a huge nose in the middle, I knew that, whatever else, he was not a mongol, and he was so big and strong there was little doubt that he was going to be all right. Perhaps this birth, and that of the third boy who was also normal, did more good than any amount of counselling or social service provision. Failing to produce a normal child the first time meant that we felt that we would never be able to do it. This fear struck very deeply at our wish to be alive and to be sure of a kind of continuity. A child gives one a place in history and in time, and there is not much that can compensate if one loses out on that.

After our second and third sons were born the problems became administrative rather than emotional. All three children were bad at sleeping but the moment we asked for a tranquilliser for David our nights became less disturbed and with better sleep greater vitality also returned. I still wonder why we had to ask for the tranquilliser and why it was not suggested as a matter of course. We have felt all along that suggestions and help have not been forthcoming readily enough. It may well be still the same assumption ('because you are intelligent') that has made social workers steer clear of offering help. Perhaps we are so used to 'self-help' that it looks as if we have no problems, but I would ask all those who come into contact with families who have mentally handicapped children in them to probe carefully and see what the difficulties are.

The greatest help was the training centre. It was suggested to us that we might try to get David in before he was five and we took him to see the principal. David immediately climbed on her desk and roared round the office; she understood straight away what it was like coping with him at home, and

offered to take him. To have David away from home between
nine and four was our greatest relief. We are sure that the
school has helped him to become better able to live in the
family. Over the years there has been real progress. It has been
slow but suddenly we realize that he can do things that we
never thought he would be able to do. He can now speak a
number of words. Perhaps the greatest breakthrough was when
he learnt what 'Yes' meant. First he could nod in assent and
now he actually says 'Yes'. This meant the end of endless
temper tantrums due to frustration. How were we to guess
that he wanted orange juice when we gave him toast? Then we
would become angry because he just threw it all on the floor.
Now he is ten and he can be much more cooperative, and this
makes a sort of benevolent circle — he is better tempered, so
we become more tolerant; he is more affectionate, so we can
return affection. There are still frightful messes. He can be
dreadfully single-minded: if he wants to do something it is not
easy to distract him or to stop him. He enjoys emptying
buckets of water on to the pavement and after a time a
situation develops that reminds us of the 'Sorcerer's
Apprentice' — water everywhere. Then we have to be firm,
that leads to a tantrum in turn, and then I become angry. I
hate the thought of bringing up children to unquestioning
obedience or squashing their initiative, but then I am always
doing what conflicts with all our beliefs. At times I feel that I
am very authoritarian with David. All the earlier fears and
disappointments well up and I become uncontrollably angry
with him. Last Christmas he climbed up to the top of the
house and dropped our second son Simon's Lego engine right
to the bottom. It exploded into all its component parts and
was broken, fortunately not beyond repair. I rushed upstairs
and slapped him so hard that my hand hurt, I then felt awful
and wanted to make it up to him but I could not do it.

His relationship with his younger brothers is obviously
complex; they are absolutely devoted to him although he
spoils their games and he can hurt them. Perhaps he is an ideal
brother: he is worse at everything they can do and he does not
represent the challenge of an older 'superior' sibling. To our
second boy, Simon, he gives security. He has said: 'I can't go

to sleep without David, he protects me from nightmares'. On many mornings we have found one or other child in David's bed where they have crept for comfort. When the boys were very small I was always afraid that David might harm them and my wife thinks that these fears were quite realistic; she never felt able to leave him with another baby and even now he is quite capable of dangerous tricks. He thinks it is a huge joke to give a little push while someone is going down the stairs in front of him. But there are other times when he can be very funny and he amuses all of us when he dances or sings a nursery rhyme. He can paint in the manner of Jackson Pollock and lately has drawn figures that have faces and feet. He used to run away which was of course dreadfully worrying, but now we can let him go into the square where he can sit literally for hours watching leaves fall or raindrops evaporating. Many neighbours accept him as an amusing oddity and in the house of friends he just walks in, helps himself to biscuits and turns on the record player!

Over the years David has become a very important member of the family. But we can't look after him for ever and his eventual removal will worry the other two. We can't take such a step lightly. Lately he has learnt to cope with going into temporary care in the residential unit: he comes home a bit restless but he is certainly not disturbed. This unit has enabled us to have holidays with the other two boys and this again has helped to lessen tension.

I have compiled this book because I feel that the needs of parents are not sufficiently understood. Time and time again the parents to whom I talked recounted difficulties like my own — they received no advice, or they would not hear it, and their burden of guilt was like my own. I marvel at the people who write about their handicapped children saying that they found help through their faith or their churches. No parent I interviewed mentioned this as a help but of course they may just have felt shy at mentioning such a thing at an interview. At a time when belonging to an official religious body and attending church is a minority activity it must be assumed that parents of mentally handicapped children will not have found any ready-made formula to see them through their troubles.

I hope some parents can use this inquiry as a point of

reference at a time when they want more than anything else to be 'normal'. They can then perhaps see that they are not unique in their reactions and that the fears and resentments they feel are shared by other people. Professional help is essential at first. Being told of the disaster, however sympathetically, is not enough. I know that psychiatrists are in short supply but I am certain that my consultation with one was an important moment. Some people may feel that psychiatrists are only useful for neurotic or other mental disturbances. I am sure that if they were available during this time of great stress, when they know the child is mentally handicapped, and if skilled counselling were available while the child is growing up, much distress could be relieved. If professional social workers could be made more aware of the needs of parents and if local authorities would set up groups where parents could talk about the problem, the sense of isolation and feelings of guilt could be lessened and much suffering could be relieved. Nothing will make the child normal but parents can be helped to cope more adequately. A social worker with a heavy case-load might find it economical in time and energy to take groups of parents rather than individuals.

Both my wife and I feel this to be an important need but under present conditions it is not easy to help. It is difficult to take the initiative at a personal level. For example, my wife saw a lady with a mongol baby in a local supermarket. She wanted to talk to her, but felt reluctant to do so since it was just possible that the mother did not know there was anything wrong with the child. In any case it is not all that easy to approach strangers. She found out from the cashier in the supermarket who the lady was, and discovered that she knew her child was a mongol; so she spoke to her and told her about a local playgroup. No one in an official position had mentioned this playgroup to the mother. Such a playgroup is of immense importance. It is not just that there is somewhere safe for the children to play, but that the mothers can talk together and exchange information.

If only we could persuade all authorities to recognize this need of parents, and to organize groups on professional lines, many burdens I have described could be shared.

CHAPTER 2
HOW THE PARENTS WERE TOLD

Now I have been under the impression all these years from the children's hospital that he had brain damage . . . they just don't tell you anything and what they do tell you is in big words and you don't understand them

My interviews show that in most cases telling the parents of their child's handicap was handled badly. But however well the telling is managed it is bound to be a great shock. As one mother said, 'I just sort of collapsed into tears, I couldn't make head or tail of anything'. When parents say they were told the news badly, they imply that they did not want to hear what they were told, and that they resented what they were forced to accept. There is no 'good' way of telling parents that their child is mentally handicapped, but there must be ways of not making a bad situation worse and of not adding to the suffering that already is bound to be considerable.

All the parents felt that they needed to have more than one meeting with whoever told them of the child's handicap. 'I think we were too shocked at the time . . . anything else he said just went into one ear and out at the other.' If the parents do not have more than one meeting with the doctor feelings of dissatisfaction will grow and misunderstanding will be inevitable. Those in authority who have to tell the parents will feel that the right thing has been done and the correct information has been given. Apart from feeling that something terrible has happened to their child the parents will be convinced that no one had told them anything and that no help whatsoever has been offered. There is a communication problem on two levels. The first is an educational problem; if a specialist is telling the parents, he may think that the information he has given them is clear and concise, but he may have assumed too much medical or general knowledge on the parents' part. It is not much use gently telling a mother that her child is a 'mongol' (or, perhaps worse, 'suffering from Down's syndrome') if the term 'mongol' does not mean anything to her. As one mother said:

My husband told me that the child was abnormal. This was a severe shock but since I knew nothing about mental handicap and had never even heard the name 'mongol' it did not really start to register for some time what the effects would be. I was naïve enough to think that perhaps some of the nurses did not know that the child was a 'mongol' and never spoke to them about it. Perhaps they were waiting for me to speak about it, and since I didn't, no help was really forthcoming. One of the sisters was quite good and helped a bit, especially with early feeding difficulties. Also the ward sister managed to empty the ward that I was in and left me on my own which was very nice: so I didn't have the constant nag of other people in the ward with normal babies wanting to discuss and admire their own babies when I didn't feel like discussing and admiring mine . . . .

A specialist came to see John when he was about ten days old; she was very reassuring and very nice. I had been warned that she would probably be very brusque with the parents. I wouldn't dream of abandoning a child, but we were warned that she seemed to think that parents would abandon their handicapped babies at the drop of a hat and that she therefore had to impress on them that they should take their babies and how normally they could be treated and how normally they would behave.

I think she underestimates parents to some extent, although obviously she is trying to do her best by the child. I don't think many parents would, if they were given a straight choice of leaving their baby in the hospital or taking it away with them, actually leave it, and if they felt so strongly that they were prepared to leave it, then it would probably be better both for the child and the parents if they were allowed to leave it than take it home and struggle with it. I think it is quite wrong that anybody should withhold this vital information, and I don't remember ever being told this. Although in fact both my husband and I were in such an emotional state that it is quite possible that we may have been told this and just not heard it.

Mrs Hopkins was treated with every possible sympathy but in the last resort felt, that although everyone had been kind, no one had actually helped her. The specialist seemed to think that parents 'would abandon their babies at the drop of a hat'. Surely to help parents keep their babies they must be allowed to express their ambivalent feelings towards the child? The assumption behind the specialist's approach may have been not to tell the parents too soon because the shock might induce them to reject the child completely. A dilemma arises here; either one increases the parents' anxiety and self-doubt by not telling them anything or one bowls them over with immediate and brusque information and assumes that all will be sorted out by a competent social worker later. I wonder whether we are not dealing with the specialist's own need for a defence against pain and suffering here. The specialist had a strong moral conviction that babies should not be abandoned by their parents but this conviction overrode the need of the mother to work through rejection of the child to acceptance.

Even if the mother knows something about the child's particular handicap, doctors should not be blinded to the fact that this in no way lessens the shock. Indeed ignorance may be bliss and the mother who can immediately start to understand the complexity of the problem may be in a much deeper state of shock. As Mrs Mercer said:

[they] started to tell me all about it. Well, I suppose I made sort of intelligent noises because I did know what mongolism was. I knew vaguely about the extra chromosomes. I knew the outward signs; but of course when they left me I just broke down completely . . . .

Secondly, the doctor may not be fully aware how much anxiety the parents are experiencing and how deep the shock may be; he simply may not realize that what he says is not heard and cannot be assimilated at that stage.

I felt unreal, that this could not be me, that if I switched off and went back to sleep, I would wake and find I had dreamed it. I even did not want to see my husband in a way, because that would have meant facing reality.

Anyone who feels anxious will be so controlled by these feelings that the information which is supposed to comfort him will not register. This is a common problem in schools where teachers at first frighten the children in order to gain control, and are then surprised when the children won't learn anything even though they are quiet. The Jenkins are a case in point:

Mrs Jenkins Well they told us at the hospital . . . we went back when he was six weeks old, didn't we? We realized something was amiss, we hadn't any idea what it was and all they said was that he had mongol tendencies.
CLH Did you go together?
Mrs Jenkins Yes, together. He examined Peter at the time. I had never known anything like it; so I didn't know what to expect at all . . . I can't really remember; I think we were too shocked at the time that anything else he said just went into one ear and out the other.

Eventually parents will want to go over the bad news again and again and this requires patient and sympathetic listeners. There is no doubt that some people are 'naturals' when they talk to someone with a problem — so that a person feels he has been helped and that he has been understood. Empathy can be increased by training and this could form part of medical and social-work training. We found this quality among friends and with some doctors. This kind of sympathy must remain distinct from pity. When the parents sense that there is pity and, as they may unreasonably suspect, condescension, they will withdraw and become resentful.

One wonders whether the telling of the news should be left to doctors at all. Most medical students are not sufficiently prepared for the fact that they will have to communicate bad news. Their course takes place during a time of their lives when they are acquiring emotional maturity and working through their own problems. The aspiring doctor is so busy accumulating factual information and mechanical skills that he has little time for the psychological aspects of medicine. Perhaps training should include simulation exercises based on the sort of material presented here. Role-playing may increase the student's perception of what is happening to the parent by increasing his self-knowledge and sensitivity. To be able to examine and experience the defences against painful reality may also give doctors some clue as to why they handle the parents of mentally handicapped children in the way they do. It is important that the parents do not lose faith in the medical profession or at a later stage they will not seek as much help for themselves or the child as they might, and may remain unable to hear and understand what the doctor has to say to them.

Mary is now four; she had her first serious fit when she was two, and was rushed to the doctor who told the parents to give her an aspirin. Later a test was made and the parents were told that she had a normal brain and that there was nothing to worry about. As the development of speech was rather slow the parents become more and more worried and again consulted with doctors, but again they were told that there was nothing seriously wrong and that if they were worried about speech they should see a speech therapist.

Then Mary had a prolonged fit and was admitted to hospital. Mr and Mrs Peters were told together that the child was brain-damaged. It was mentioned that she might be no more than a 'cabbage' for the rest of her life. Mr Peters felt it was right that he had been told the worst immediately — it was a hard shock but he always wanted to know the worst straight away. For Mrs Peters it was a different matter. She had a nervous breakdown for the next six months, blamed herself for what happened, and could not sleep at night because she was (and is) afraid that Mary would have a fit in her sleep. Mr Peters thought it was cruel the way his wife had been told.

No one will ever know whether Mrs Peters's nervous breakdown was entirely caused by the news that the child was mentally handicapped, but of the parents interviewed, two of the mothers said that they had had nervous breakdowns and one father's stay in a psychiatric ward was said to be because of the child. It would be rash on the basis of one interview with each family to suggest what exactly caused the mental illness of the parents but surely it is clear that the parents of mentally handicapped children are at considerable risk. The news tests their resilience and personality to the limit and the need for support should be recognized. Mr Peters saw himself as the 'male' and 'tough' member of the family and thought it was right that he had been told; Mrs Peters was cast in the weak and feminine role and was allowed at least the 'luxury' of breaking down. The man had to carry the burden: he then suffered a serious accident at work and has been ill for quite some time.

Like the Peters family, Mr and Mrs Richards suffered greatly because the child was brain-damaged. The father was still unable to accept the fact that he had a handicapped child and the family must have presented a grave problem to the visiting social worker. As the child was brain-damaged and not a mongol there was the additional problem that all this was not immediately apparent (although, in fact, Mrs Richards suspected immediately that something **was** wrong, without knowing exactly what it was). A mongol, on the other hand, can be spotted straight away but other defects take time and the telling of it may then come as an even greater shock.

Mrs Richards She had enormous hands and feet and she had giantism, and then, you know, they couldn't tell us an awful lot. They said they didn't know themselves . . . The doctor delivered her and was there at the birth and signed both of us as fit and normal — the baby normal! She didn't seem to think there was anything wrong.
CLH When did your husband know that something was the matter? Did you talk to him straight away or did he notice?
Mrs Richards No, I don't think so. I think perhaps he did, but my husband was reluctant to accept it, you know, recognize it; in fact he hasn't accepted it yet, that's why he is in hospital now . . . a week after they told us, he went down with pneumonia, his lung collapsed and he hasn't worked since and they thought it was due to the shock. He has gradually gone down and he is in a psychiatric ward now . . . He does talk about it, but I don't think he can quite accept it. He resents anyone telling him that there is something wrong with Jill.
CLH Who told him?
Mrs Richards Well, health visitors and people like this. I dread them coming to the house because it always ends up with either the visitors just walking out in disgust or my husband telling them to go out. It has caused quite a lot of problems in the family . . . .

One parent felt that the family's own doctor was the best person to break the news. The doctor probably knows the family better than anyone at the hospital and may be able to judge more sensitively how to go about telling the parents. However it will not always be possible for the doctor to be involved in this way.

Mrs Mercer again states all the dilemmas: should the parents be told sooner or later? Separately or together? Should the parents be told that they need not take the child home? Is this an ethical or socially acceptable alternative?

Mrs Mercer When he was only three days old I suspected there
was something wrong with him. I could see that his eyes were
a bit funny and I kept asking people around me. I asked a nurse
in the hospital and that very evening I had the paediatrician
down and my first thought was: why have they waited so
long to tell me? The doctor and a junior paediatrician came
charging down to my bedside after my husband had gone and
started to tell me all about it. Well I suppose I made sort of
intelligent noises . . . but of course when they left me I just
broke down completely . . . I was just wailing I think;
eventually I just sobbed that I wanted my husband, and he
came straight back. Of course the poor man couldn't
understand what it was all about, having left me fit, well and
healthy. That's the only thing I have to criticize.

CLH You said earlier no one knows how to handle the telling
of the news that something is wrong with the child.

Mrs Mercer I think the father should be there too. I think it's a
little unfair to tell him by himself, and have him knowing, you
know; it's an added strain having to keep something away
from the wife if you think she is not fit to bear it.

CLH Would you be in favour of sooner rather than later?

Mrs Mercer Yes, although I've heard many people say that you
would want the wife physically to get over the birth. My
argument is that this news knocks you right back again
anyway, you might as well have the two together and get them
out of the way entirely. It's something you have got to learn
to live with. I was told that there were three mongol children
in the hospital perfectly fit and healthy, their parents just
refused to have them at home, and none of them had been
told until the child was getting on a bit, and she [the doctor]
thought, she still does, that the longer you leave telling the
parents the more likely it is that they will reject them.

CLH Was it ever indicated to you that you might, as an
alternative, put this child into hospital straight away?

Mrs Mercer No, never. No one ever suggested that there was
any alternative at all, and I certainly couldn't have walked
away and left him in hospital.

Mrs Mercer's son was three days old when they told her that he was mentally handicapped. Clearly she was very upset by the news and would have welcomed her husband's support at that very difficult moment. In fact, her husband was sent for as she was so distraught. For only one partner to know about the handicap is obviously a great strain, whether it is the father or mother.

Many parents were critical of the type and amount of information they were given when news of their child's handicap was broken to them. I think it must be accepted that there will often be anger and resentment directed against the teller of the bad news because he will always be associated with it and may always remain a part of the angry feelings aroused at the time. If the doctor can accept these feelings without becoming resentful and punitive he may in time be able to work through them with the parents. If, on the other hand, the feelings of the parents remain too strong and hostile it may be necessary to change doctors and talk about the problem to someone else.

When faced with the task of telling parents that their child is handicapped the doctor may already suspect that the parents know something is wrong. This complicates the situation. One family I interviewed already knew that their child was a mongol before they were told; the wife had worked in a child-health department and could recognize her son's abnormality by his face. Other parents felt that something was 'not quite right' about their baby, sometimes without being able to pinpoint just what this was. This was the case with Mrs Mercer (see p. 31). However, some parents will realize that something is wrong but will not admit the fact, and try to convince themselves that they are worrying unnecessarily. Praising, or possibly overpraising the baby's progress can raise false hopes, as Mrs Shepherd found (see p. 33).

The trouble with waiting until the parent asks is that by the time this happens the parents know already — or they have a fair degree of certainty. The parent often knows much more than he or she lets on and, in order to avoid a painful confrontation, both sides of the 'game' collude and pretend there is no problem. For the doctor this is the least painful approach but it must be remembered that the parents have suffered agonies of doubt and uncertainty, often in complete isolation.

Mr and Mrs Shepherd waited six months before they were told their son was handicapped. During that time they suspected something was wrong but 'it was a case of; if no one puts in into words it can't happen'. They had broached the subject indirectly at the clinic after a couple of months, but in spite of voicing worries about feeding difficulties and general lack of progress, their son was six months old when they **themselves** asked if their little boy was a mongol . . . and were told that this was the case.

Mr Shepherd We found that they left telling us much too long. A couple of months, three months, well fair enough, but when we started asking questions, once or twice she approached the doctor and said, you know, he isn't eating and he isn't doing this and he isn't sucking his bottle as well as he should, well then was the time that we should have been told, when we were inquiring and worrying that he wasn't progressing properly, and knowing too that my wife had been working with young children.

Mrs Shepherd I think they probably tried to sound you out; I took him in when he was about three months and she was talking to him and holding him and his eyes were lighting up a little bit and she said, 'He is quite a bright boy for three months, isn't he?' Well now, instead of reacting as she hoped I would and saying 'Well now, I am rather worried', I clutched at that as a drowning man would at a straw and said 'Thank God, there can't be anything wrong with him', and didn't say anything and just went home . . . I do think over this, if you have a good understanding doctor, I think he is the best person to tell you, really, but as I said, we only had a young inexperienced one, and were rather unlucky.

Some of the parents I interviewed had been told together about their child's handicap, while in other cases either the wife or the husband had been told alone, leaving them to break the news to their spouse.

Mr Davis was told his son was a mongol and advised not to tell his wife straight away; however, like many married couples he decided that it would be impossible to keep the news from her and so went and broke it to her that evening.

Mr Davis Well, first of all, very shortly after Christopher was born, the doctor at the nursing home called me into his room and told me that the sister in the hospital had an idea that Christopher would not be a normal child. My immediate reaction was: 'Well if he is going to be abnormal in any way, I hope he dies.' The doctor also told me that I had better not tell my wife at this stage; however, I went out of the room and straight in to see my wife and, as I believe married people do who live fairly happily together, she sort of read my face and said 'What's wrong?' and in spite of the doctor telling me not to tell her, I did.

Mrs Davis I had been to see Christopher and I took one look at him and I knew he was a mongol, I could just tell by the shape of his face. It was easier then, I was glad someone else had told my husband because I didn't want to have to.

Many, if not all the parents will wish at some time that the child had died. As most of us love life and feel strongly that it should be preserved at almost any cost, this is a shocking thought. Rather than make these feelings of guilt become unbearable and secret it is essential that they are allowed to come out and be accepted as natural. If the parent has wished the child dead it is no use going into pious sermons on the sanctity of life. It is better that these feelings of ambivalence are expressed rather than suppressed. Once they have been worked through it may be easier for the parents to accept the child for what he is.

Parents can work through these feelings, as Mr and Mrs Davis did:

We both hoped he would die because he was very, very ill, but they sort of fought tooth and nail to save him, and they did, and when he was over the bad bout we both said, 'If he is going to live let's take him home as quickly as possible and do what we can for him'.

It is not unusual for parents to have fantasies about murdering their handicapped child and it is important that these thoughts, which are very disturbing to the parents, are talked through, so that in talking about them feelings of guilt and shame may be relieved. It is rare for a parent to kill a handicapped child but many parents fear that they will do something violent to the child. If these fears can be expressed without moral censure the tension may lessen and the nagging wish to harm one's own child may be understood as a natural reaction which is common to most people and not the result of unique wickedness.

A moral approach to parents; telling them what they **ought** to feel and assuming that all children will automatically be loved, is unwise — it will only make them feel worse. They will no longer reveal their genuine feelings and they will avoid discussing the problem altogether. Obviously one would hope that eventually the child will come to be accepted, but not everyone can achieve this. As Mrs Richards said:

My husband was very reluctant to accept it . . . to recognize it; he does talk about it, but I don't think he can quite accept it. He resents anyone telling him that there is something wrong with Jill.

Mrs Williams's boy is now eight and she is not at all clear what is the matter with him. She does not seem to have understood the methods of diagnosis or the results. Here is a clear example of almost total lack of communication between middle-class doctors, social workers and a working-class mother who is intelligent, but anxious and upset.

Mrs Williams I first noticed that he had fits when he was nine months old; we didn't have a doctor when we first moved out here. I took him to the casualty in the children's hospital. From then on he was up there, he had blood tests and everything, and when he was a year and three months he had his first double EEG; then, by the time he was two years of age, I knew then there was something wrong with him.

CLH Did somebody take you aside and tell you about this?
Mrs Williams No.
CLH How did you find out?
Mrs Williams This is just something that I found out for myself.

I have already mentioned how the anxiety of the parents and lack of experience or insensitivity on the part of the doctor can make communication between the two sides very difficult.

Although it is clear that not many parents reject their mentally handicapped child completely, one mother was particularly upset that she and her husband had not been told that they could leave the child at the hospital, should they feel unable to accept it and care for it. Clearly the doctor wants the best deal for the child, but this should not override consideration for the parents' needs and feelings: they should be treated as adults and allowed to see the alternatives. It is extremely important that the situation is outlined realistically and that the parents are told what can be and what cannot be done for the child. It is unrealistic for the doctor to assume that all this will be done by the social worker. Feelings can't be split into departments: the doctor can't be the one who deals with 'facts' and the social worker the one who deals with 'feelings'.

A survey conducted in London in 1964, quoted in the introduction to Barbara Furneaux's **The Special Child**, stated that 'in many instances the communication of the discovery of mental defect was handled badly'. Sadly I found this still to be true. How, and at what stage, to tell the parents is one of the most difficult problems facing doctors. Some may feel that if parents are told too soon after the birth the shock will induce them to reject the child; others will feel that to wait, while the parents' anxiety and self-doubt pile up, is to make the task even more difficult and increases the chances of parental rejection. Whatever doctors decide to do they should be aware of their own defences, which may make them decide on a course that is easier for them to tolerate than one which just meets the needs of the parents.

Comments and recommendations

1 It is the parents' right to know that the child is handicapped and they should be told by a competent person as soon as possible after the birth. Where the medical staff **suspect** that a handicap exists, the parents should be informed, whether or not they have asked. Bland reassurances do not convince an anxious parent. An honest assessment should be given, allowing time for the parents to absorb information and to understand it.

2 Medical students should have more extensive training in conveying bad news to their patients. This is part of treatment. From my interviews it seemed to many parents that doctors sometimes made incomprehensible statements and then withdrew from the scene. This may not have been what the doctors thought they were doing, but that was how it **seemed** to the parents. Most parents want an adult discussion and don't want 'things' to be decided for them behind their backs. However, it is important that doctors do not talk so 'technically' that parents do not understand the information being given.

3 Advice given should be repeated. It must not be assumed that one session with an articulate professional is enough. A sensitive and competent social worker should work with the family doctor, who is the best person to see that the family does not become isolated and the mother depressed. Advice given without making sure that it has been heard and assimilated is not very useful.

4 Parents will often say: 'no one ever tells us anything', 'no one understands'. These must be understood for what they are: cries for **help.**

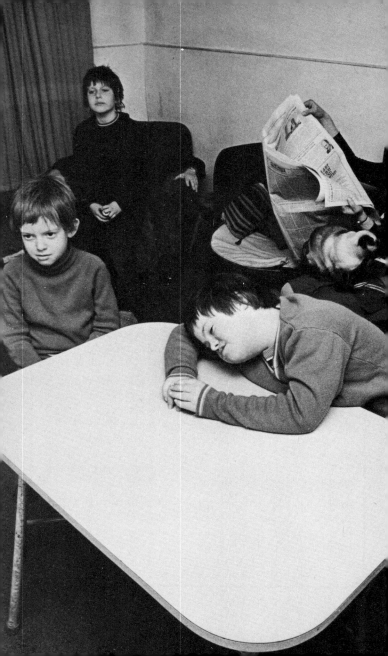

CHAPTER 3
THE EFFECT ON FAMILY LIFE

My wife and I do snap at each other occasionally,
but we have got a little accelerator
in the house that causes provocations

All families cope with disasters differently; there are the 'solids' who have resource enough in themselves to cope and who can fall back on other members of the family, whose relationships are lasting and cannot be disturbed; and there are the 'brittles', who are shattered and helpless and need much support from outside agencies. Probably we all fall between these two extremes. Because extended families are not as close as they used to be, and families tend to live apart, another source of support and help is lost.

Not that all mothers and mothers-in-law are an ideal source of help. Mr and Mrs Shepherd describe very vividly the unease the younger generation can feel when in contact with the older. The neighbours are often not all that much use and again one does not always want to go on asking for help. They can be relied on in an absolute emergency, as when Mrs Shepherd had to run to the doctor.

When there are small children as well as the mentally handicapped child there is always the fear that this child will harm the others. Mrs Hopkins was in this quandary and she quite realistically feared for the safety of her children. The Shepherds explain one of the difficulties they have with babysitters. It is one thing to ask someone just to sit in, but quite another to expect them to deal with soiled bedding.

Mr Shepherd Fortunately in my job I don't have to bring work home with me, but now there is a five-day week . . . no, I don't find any strain with him in relation to my job. We have just had our holiday; well we have solved that now, you see, with the hostel [the local special school has a residential unit attached to it] ; this solves our holiday problem, we have always felt before we have never gone away much apart from relatives . . .
Mrs Shepherd My husband has mentioned relatives. We have found that this is getting very difficult now; it isn't quite so bad going to my husband's mother — she will give the children practically anything — but we went to **my** mother last August, and she was a bit fussy. We found it was very difficult right from the word go. With meals he tends to go all over the place and she insists that you have him right up to the table and it's very

difficult, and in the end we found that the only way we could cope was for one of us to stay with him in the room all the time, so that if my husband wanted to leave the room he had to get me from somewhere to stay with Stephen. We didn't tell my parents this, obviously, because they would have been upset. They thought they were giving us a restful week but it wasn't really, you know.

Mr Shepherd I think our biggest problem is that we have nobody around in the family. All our neighbours are pretty good, they can do certain things . . . .

Mrs Shepherd When you say they are pretty good, love, they aren't really; no one will actually have him. Our next-door neighbour will have him for half-an-hour while I run to the doctor's, and I mean run, but no, no one has ever . . . the doctor did give me a bottle of dope that we could give Stephen if we ever wanted anyone to babysit, and we do sometimes go to the pictures and we give him some of this medicine and then we just go to see the big film. We leave at about eight p.m. and come straight back. Once every two months at the most.

CLH What stops you from going out?

Mr Shepherd Really, it is getting someone to babysit. Most of our friends rely on youngsters, schoolchildren, and we don't honestly feel we can leave him.

Mrs Shepherd It isn't only that you see, he gets — he did go through a phase a lot where he persistently had his bowels open in the evening, or worse, he would start to half change himself and the bed would be in a mess and I loathe the idea of neighbours having to clean up after him because I don't like having to do it myself, now he is eight, and so I didn't ask . . . but quite honestly we haven't had anyone to babysit at all, have we, the next-door neighbour or . . .

CLH Does this mean you go out in turns?

Mrs Shepherd No, it means we just don't go out at all. We go out as a family at weekends, but in the week we stay at home; as I say once every couple of months . . . After Stephen had his tonsils out, he couldn't go out. You see if Stephen can't go out then I am tied to the house completely, I mean I can't even go shopping.

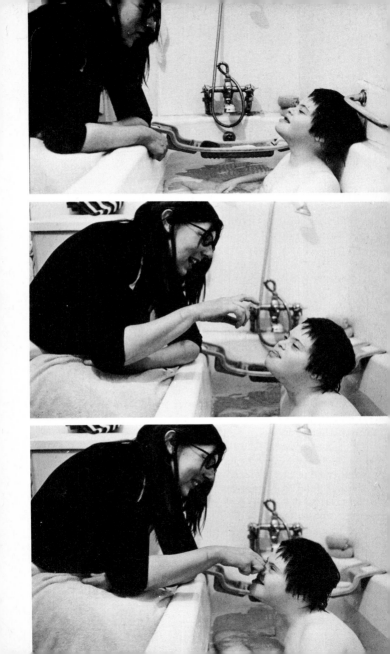

Mr and Mrs Davis mention the feeling of tiredness, a point which in fact came up in every interview. This is not just the tiredness after a hard day's work, but a sense of total exhaustion and depression that comes of an accumulation of bad nights, irritation and 'just coping'. Not enough energy is left for going out in the evenings and getting away.

Mr Davis I think the strain is that I am managing a large organization; by the end of a week sometimes I am pretty weary mentally, and I feel sometimes Monday morning that the weekend has been a dead loss from my own selfish angle. That's because relationships in the house have been strained, perhaps because of a broken night's sleep, perhaps he has been naughty. At the same time it is a routine one gets very used to, and I kid myself that as I get older and have these [management] responsibilities I get a bit tougher mentally . . . my wife and I do snap at each other occasionally. It's what we would do normally, but we have got a little accelerator in the house that causes provocations.

Mrs Davis I can always dig up a babysitter . . . but we both get physically very tired. I just can't be bothered.

CLH What about your family?

Mr Davis My mother is extremely fond of Christopher but she only comes once a year, perhaps for a long weekend . . . .

Mrs Davis And she has become extremely interested in mentally-handicapped children now. She takes a great interest and is very good with him.

Mr Davis At work I suppose all the senior people know that I have a mentally-handicapped boy, but he is never referred to, that is except by my secretary who has been to the house and knows the circumstances.

Mrs Davis My parents are dead now, but my sisters are not really interested; they all live a long way away. One of my sisters came to stay last year and she was sympathetic and made a lot of inquiries. She thinks that Christopher ought to be taught to talk. I said people can't make them talk . . . She is concerned for him, but the rest of my sisters, I think they feel that they have their own families and problems. We were a big family.

As with any children, the main burden falls on the mothers. The fathers can at least get away to work, and by immersing themselves in it forget the problems at home for a while. For the mothers there is no escape unless outsiders come and help or the child can go to a residential unit occasionally. Now that training centres have become part of the education service, ordinary school holidays have been introduced. This puts an added burden on the family. Holidays are surely essential for the teachers and staff but the mentally handicapped child at home must make life very difficult for the parents. Playgroups and residential units are a great help in holidays and these are dealt with in later chapters.

The break in the routine caused by the holidays upsets the children and affects their sleeping, feeding and toilet-training. Unless there is a babysitter, such 'normal' activities as shopping, hair-cutting for the other children and changing library books, become so unpleasant a hazard that they are dropped as far as possible when the handicapped child is at home. The family's activities are geared to the handicapped child's capabilities. There is no choice about this and everyone else has to go to the wall.

Comments and recommendations

1 A babyminding service for housebound parents, particularly mothers, is needed. Perhaps this could be part of the home-help organization. Part of the difficulty is the expense of having continually to find and use a minder for the most ordinary occasions. There are many places to which a mother cannot take her mentally handicapped child because of the disturbance he may create. For example: supermarkets, libraries, even a visit to the clinic with another child can be a severe trial; one has to be watchful all the time. Even housework becomes more difficult. For these reasons extra help is essential if the mother is to lead any sort of normal life.

2 The present arrangement for opening and staffing schools for mentally handicapped children only partially meets the needs of the parents and children. If hospitals can stay open all the year round so can schools. Obviously the staff need adequate holidays so this would mean additional staff. While one realizes that voluntary help has its limitations, here seems a good opportunity to use it.

3 The Attendance Allowance should be paid to **all** parents of mentally handicapped children who live at home. This would enable parents to pay for help in the home, either for cleaning or to look after the handicapped child.

4 Sleep is vital for the morale and well-being of the family. Every effort should be made to make sure that the family gets a good night's sleep, if necessary with the help of tranquillizing drugs.

5 If taking the child on holiday presents difficulties, a short period in a residential unit can give the parents a much-needed break.

CHAPTER 4
PARENTS AND OTHER PEOPLE

I'd take him anywhere with me; if people don't like it, it's up to them to close their ears and walk away. He's got a right to be on this earth as much as they have

Having a baby is usually an occasion for rejoicing and much public congratulation. The new baby is paraded in the pram, everyone likes to have a look and coo over it and the parents can glow with pleasure and satisfaction. All babies seem to be beautiful, at least to other mothers, and there is the feeling of having created something perfect, a sense of continuity and the belief that a bit of oneself will live on for the future.

There is of course another side to having babies: depression, anti-climax and loss of freedom, but these are not the aspects that come out in public. When the birth has gone badly and the child is mentally handicapped this is a tremendous blow to the self-esteem of the parents; they have either failed or been singled out by fate. All the feelings of guilt and inadequacy are heightened, and there is a sense of 'failure' and a 'spoiled identity'.

Mrs Mercer is one such parent who expresses these feelings. She fears both rejection and sympathy. This makes it very difficult for other people to help, and very often the result is either too much sympathy or just a denial of any sort of problem. Mrs Mercer thinks she 'bored people to tears'; in fact just listening was probably the greatest help they were able to give her.

Mrs Mercer They came in to see the baby and each one that came in I said to them 'Do you know about him?' and all held out their arms and said 'Of course we do', 'Let me hold him'. But I did find difficulty in going out, although I did ask a friend of mine who lived across the road to tell everybody that I knew, so that I didn't have that awful feeling of suddenly while I am out somebody haring over and saying 'How's the new baby?', looking down and saying 'Ugh'. You know, she told everybody, but I couldn't face the thought of seeing people and this went on for about six weeks.

CLH Were you afraid of sympathy?

Mrs Mercer Yes. I'd get ready and I'd think, this is silly, and I'd put on my coat and my lipstick and then I'd get the baby in the pram, then I'd take my coat off and send the children down to the shops; and, as I say, my husband goes out for a drink every night, and the first time I plucked up courage to go with him, I could see Bill over by the bar, and I smiled, a sort of tentative smile, and I could see his face drop, and I could see the sympathy coming out. He started across the bar towards me and I had to hare out into the ladies and have a little weep, and my husband sent someone in to me. I plonked on lots of powder and said 'It's all right, but it's Bill', and my husband went back and had a word with Bill and said 'For God's sake don't say anything' and gave me a stiff whisky and I felt a lot better, but I think it's people's sympathy that I was afraid of meeting.

Well, all of my friends were willing to listen; I must have bored them to tears and I think if I hadn't been able to I'd have gone nuts, looking back . . . I remember the first party we went to after Philip was born. There were all these people I hadn't seen for a long time and I felt they all knew about Philip and they were all saying 'Have you heard about it, poor soul' and I stood there with a glass in my hand and my hand was shaking and then this silly woman came over and said Are you feeling all right, my dear? You look pale and you're shaking' and I thought, you know, nobody understands how difficult it is to be normal.

Mr and Mrs Peters show that the brain-damaged child presents a particular problem, for it is not obvious just by looking at many to see that there is something wrong. After all, a mongol in most cases is very markedly a mongol and people will make allowances; but a child with a damaged brain will behave oddly, which makes it harder to bear: outsiders will not make immediate allowances for the strange behaviour of a child who looks so normal.

While outwardly there is nothing wrong with Mary ('she is a beautiful child'), her behaviour is difficult. She will do naughty things impulsively, and in shops and other places the parents have been told that what the child needs is a good smacking. Both parents have been very upset because there have been remarks like that in the shop on the corner and by neighbours. Mr Peters had to go and tell people about the brain-damage, and he has found that hard to do. It is even worse for Mrs Peters, who is terribly upset if the child's brain-damage is talked about. To her, it is particularly annoying when people on television, for the sake of a joke, call each other half-witted and feeble-minded.

Mrs Williams had difficulties with the neighbours and finds at times that she is put on the defensive, particularly by car-owners who are touchy about their property.

Mrs Williams But anyway, there's one chap down the road, he's got a mobile van and since he's been in the street it's absolute murder with him. 'Cos nobody must even look at his van. Well, Bobby got this habit of going and touching his mirrors; well, I think a few weeks back the man said Bobby was playing with an iron bar. All it was was just a little bar, and he came up and he played hell with me. And I wasn't even here when it happened. My husband was supposed to be looking after him.

On the other hand, other neighbours were understanding and helpful.

Mrs Williams Well, the holidays are the worst time. Bobby will be out on the roads and he's up and down touching people's cars. He broke an aerial off a chap's car next door He never came and said to me 'Here's the bill'; which was very nice of him. I had a marvellous neighbour. She used to take him off for the day for me, especially when I was going through what I call a 'really bad stage'.
CLH This was when the third boy was born, I expect.
Mrs Williams Yes, now this is what I call the really worst. I know I had bad times before but this was really the worst. Oh, my neighbour walked in here one day and I had Bobby by the throat; well I would have strangled him. And she said, 'Put his coat on and I'll take him out'. But if it hadn't been for that neighbour one of us would have been done in, either me or him.
CLH When he was small, what helped you, how did you get over the shock?

Mr Jenkins There's not much difference with Peter anyway.
He is a high-grade mongol and we just treated him as normal . . .
I've got a picture of him here actually; it's not very
noticeable now, being a mongol, he hasn't got distinct mongol
features which helps.
CLH What about the family?
Mr Jenkins Well they probably showed him a lot more
affection.
CLH Did they help you with the problems?
Mr Jenkins Well, I don't think we showed that we had a
problem to be quite honest . . . We felt we were coping, but we
didn't have anything to compare with, we just went along.
CLH What about neighbours?
Mr Jenkins I don't think a lot of people realized at the time.
Mrs Jenkins They probably did, but they didn't say anything
to us.
Mr Jenkins People don't say anything about it, do they?
Mrs Jenkins No, they don't come right out and say it.
Mr Jenkins You don't really know what they are thinking, do
you?
Mrs Jenkins Everyone was very kind actually.
CLH Would it have helped if someone had talked about it?
Mrs Jenkins I don't know, I couldn't bring myself to at that
stage.
Mr Jenkins We find it easier to do it now . . . .

Mrs Shepherd describes herself as 'not very much stiff-
upper-lip' and she seems to find it easy to help others to talk
about the problem. Once it is clear that parents of mentally
handicapped children can talk about their children others find
it much easier to take the cue and ask questions. Often there is
a considerable reluctance to take an initiative because of the
fear of hurting feelings.

There is a reverse side to the coin: some comfort offered is
so tactless that one must suspect either deep ignorance or
aggression. Both Mrs Hopkins and Mrs Shepherd have suffered
because of such hurtful remarks. Mongols are not significantly
more musical or affectionate than other children, but they

have been given these stereotyped virtues which are continually offered as some sort of comfort. Thanks to the efforts of the National Society for Mentally Handicapped Children and sympathetic treatment by the mass media, mental handicap is no longer a disgrace and it is talked about more openly. But it is clear from the interviews that parents felt themselves to be the objects of pity and tactless remarks, which probably reflect the helplessness that most outsiders feel when something has gone so terribly wrong.

Mrs Shepherd We are the sort of people who go out of their way to find out what is available. The health visitor called two or three times a year, but apart from my visits to the clinic we didn't have any help at all.

CLH How did you feel at that time?

Mrs Shepherd We are not very much stiff-upper-lip people; I found it easy right from the word go to talk about it to people. I talked to a lot of people about it, it's part of our everyday life, and I can't talk about my older little girl, so I talk about Stephen, you know. It's automatic.

CLH How do they react?

Mrs Shepherd Oh most people are very kind actually.

Mr Shepherd Kind, yes . . . they overdo it sometimes. We found that some people knew before we did, and once they knew that we knew, as it were, they were quite willing to talk although we did have one or two peculiar comments from the older people.

Mrs Shepherd I started having a cleaning woman in one day a week and she said to me the other day, 'My uncle's got a mongol child and he says they are just like little monkeys', and this sort of thing. She is really a very sweet person, and you know they don't mean anything by it. It is just to be passed over. Another tactless remark we had when I had a couple of miscarriages was 'What must be wrong with you that you keep on having all these things?' This is the kind of remark that hurts me; they are numerous, and I think it is best to disregard them.

Mrs Hopkins again underlines the difficulty in telling a parent the news that her child is a mongol: it took weeks for the news to sink in, and again she found sympathy useless. Her strength lay in the fact that her husband could support her and she knew that help was available if she asked for it. What social workers and administrators have to bear in mind is that not all families have either the physical or inner resources to cope although most of the parents interviewed here had. The questions Mrs Hopkins wanted to ask came up gradually and each item had to be absorbed in turn. Right at the beginning this would have been useless, but I can imagine that a group of mothers who meet occasionally and who have available to them the services of someone who is not only well informed in matters concerning mentally handicapped children, but is skilled in counselling techniques, could do much to relieve pressure and allay at least some of the anxieties.

Mrs Hopkins After we had been to the hospital to have blood tests and had them confirmed we knew that the child was a mongol and I really began to knuckle down to the fact that I would have to live with it. This news was brought to us just after Christmas; after that there was a very heavy snowfall and we were isolated for a long time. I didn't take the baby out, even to the clinic, and not many people came to see us, they left us alone, which is perhaps the best thing they could have done. I was quite incapable of coping with sympathy. I just wanted to be left on my own: such support as I wanted came from my husband and not from my friends, who, I am sure, would have come and helped if I had asked. When John was born we had a home help, sent by the local authority, who herself had a mongol sister. It was thought that she would be able to help us more than anyone else. In fact she got on our nerves by continually hanging over the cot and making remarks like 'Isn't he lovely, not like my sister Margaret, she's ugly'. We couldn't stand her and after a time asked her to leave. We had no other help from the local authority except for occasional visits from a health visitor. Really there wasn't much she could do except give a few words of encouragement and a little practical advice.

Mrs Davis received great kindness and found that the health visitor was the greatest help. But in general, the parents feel that people 'don't seem to understand'. This feeling is so common to all of them that perhaps it needs an interpretation — it may not just mean that no one understands what the handicap is all about, but that the particular needs of the family are not understood. Inner feelings are not easy to communicate, particularly in a society like ours which still gives value to the 'stiff upper-lip' and where tenderness can still be a taboo, particularly to men.

Mrs Davis My health visitor could not have been more helpful — a very sympathetic person and very considerate of your feelings . . . for instance I was going to take him to a clinic and she said 'I wouldn't do that', and I realized after that I would have been very upset seeing all the other babies and how they were getting on. You forget how a normal child develops (my daughter was fifteen when he was born) . . . I knew that mongols don't really develop.

Mr Davis My wife is an ardent reader on any subject that interests her and she took the trouble, I know, to read many books on the subject of training and upbringing of that type of child, so that she was really confirming, stage by stage, how she should be treating the situation.

Mrs Davis I got worried that I would say things to my doctor and he would say wait, wait and see.

Mr Davis We got the impression that our doctor would prescribe for him, but he wouldn't go out of his way to meet our problems or advise us.

CLH Why was this?

Mr Davis I can't tell you, it was just a particular doctor's make-up — had children of his own, all perfectly healthy — quite a few children, so he knew all about children . . . but he never asked us how ours was getting on or whether he was making any progress. Now we have moved we have changed our doctor and he seems more interested.

Friendship without much speech is difficult but possible

CLH Have you ever talked to people who really understood what it was all about?

Mrs Davis No, people don't seem to . . . although this health visitor has been kindness itself to me . . . she has given me practical help. She retired just before the summer and she came in every day in the holidays and collected Christopher. She did this every day. She wouldn't accept anything at all. She took him out in her car, to the seaside, swimming and said 'You have a good rest' . . . she has been a very kind person but I feel I can't ask her again, you can't impose on people.

Mr Davis Nobody is unsympathetic, but nobody understands . . . .

Comments and recommendations

1 From an early age the parents must be encouraged to take the child out so that friends and neighbours can see him, can accept him and can lose their fears of mental handicap. Other children should be encouraged to play with the child; they should have explained to them the nature of the handicap and what the child can and can't do.

Mentally handicapped people arouse fears and while the National Society for Mentally Handicapped Children has done much educational work to lessen these fears, each family has to educate its neighbours. For a family that is already under a severe stress this is asking a lot, but it is easier to teach by example than just to talk about the problem in an abstract way.

2 A friend or a neighbour who takes the mentally handicapped child for a walk will do more good than one who just offers sympathy or compliments the family on how well they are coping! Having the child out of the house, even for just an hour or so, will give the mother a chance to relax.

3 Unsympathetic neighbours considerably increase the stress in the family. If the child looks normal this seems to make matters worse, because critical comments will be made more readily. The parents will have to be all the more prepared to talk about their child's handicap.

4 It is important for parents to be able to talk to other people about their child, whether those people are relatives or outside the family. It is essential for parents to be able to express openly feelings of hostility or aggression towards the handicapped child.

5 Babysitters prepared to deal with all the possible disruptions of a handicapped child would free the parents to go out together occasionally.

CHAPTER 5
BROTHERS AND SISTERS

He likes banging on his drum and makes us all go mad. He had a guitar for his birthday and he plays that. It is very difficult for Mummy and Daddy because they don't understand him

When we had our second child who was normal, a
well-meaning colleague warned me that we should have to be
careful because she knew of a family where the other children
had begun to behave like the abnormal child who had,
therefore, been put into a home. I imagine that this piece of
advice is about as valid as saying 'don't keep a dog because all
your children will bark'; on the other hand, it strikes deep and
adds to the apprehension and fears that abound. We have
certainly watched our children very carefully, constantly
looking for undue stresses and strain (and therefore probably
creating them!).

Jill Ashley Miller writes in **The Times** (11 October 1971)
about the time she had to decide whether to keep her child at
home or not: 'The wise paediatrician had said at the time of
her birth (a mongol girl), "However hard it is, always put the
normal children first".' I am sure this would be very good
advice if one knew what was best for the 'normal' children and
what is best for the family as a whole. For example, is it better
to face up to the problem of having a mentally handicapped
child together, as a family unit, or does one in a sense deny its
existence by having it removed to a home?

What I have learnt is that however difficult the child is, he
becomes an integral part of the family structure. To split this
part off, to send him to an institution, would change the
dynamics of that family's structure, and it is therefore not a
step to be taken lightly. It does seem, from these interviews at
least, that the position of the child in his family very much
influences the kind of problems that will arise. Mrs Mercer's
Philip is the youngest of six children who accept him as their
responsibility and do not like it if the parents suggest he goes
into a residential unit.

Mrs Mercer He is the youngest of six children which I think
makes it a lot easier. I have got my others who are normal;
bright kids who give me the satisfaction of their intellectual
achievements, and this one is really like having a friendly dog
around the place. We pat him on the head and spoil him . . . In
fact he doesn't talk; but I suppose we don't really stimulate

him enough at home, we give in to him too easily, but it has its advantages from my point of view in that I am not so wrapped up in him.

CLH What about the rest of the family?

Mrs Mercer Oh, they have been awfully good about it. My eldest boy, he was eleven when Philip was born, and I made my husband tell the children before I came home. I knew very well I was going to be in tears and they would ask why, so I made him tell Richard first, and Richard sat and listened to him and then he said 'Can we keep him?' In fact they have been marvellous about him and so have their friends.

CLH How do they treat him?

Mrs Mercer Indulgently. The boy who is twelve now, he got to the model-making stage at the age of six and Philip would sometimes get in the way and then of course there would be a great hoo-ha about it, but they are very fond of him, very tolerant, and very forgiving; they all look after him, too. Everybody has got their eyes and ears open for doors and things like this. The girl who is next to him in age, she is particularly fond of him. They rush into each other's arms when they have been apart for a day.

CLH Have you sent Philip to the residential unit at the centre?

Mrs Mercer No. Never. No. The main objection comes from my children. There is a great cry of 'If he were normal you wouldn't dream of doing that'. I suggested it when we were going to my niece's twenty-first birthday party; they said they could cope and I said 'No, I think I'll put Philip into the residential unit'. 'Don't you dare,' they said 'he doesn't leave until we go to school, we can wait for the bus. We are home before he comes home.' . . . We wouldn't dare put him in for a holiday because they adore playing with him on the sands. Each year they would say 'I wonder if Philip will go in this time, shall we try this with him, shall we try that with him?' We got him in last year and couldn't get him out.

Jill Richards is the youngest of five children. She causes great difficulties to her parents, and the next brother seems to suffer because of her. In these situations it is not easy to distinguish

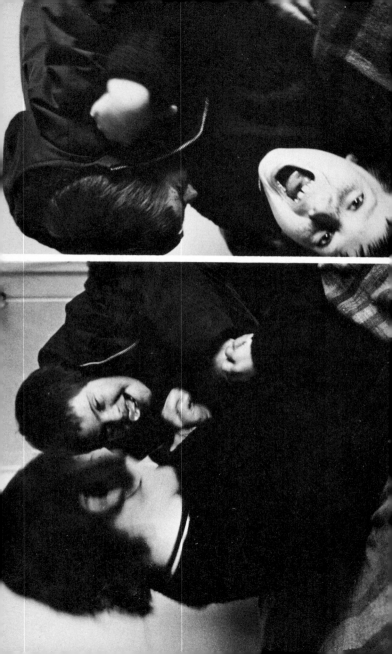

what degree of difficulty is created by the mental handicap and what is inherent in the problems of that particular family. An older sister, Sue, seems almost unaware of her sister's peculiarities: aged sixteen, she was present at the interview.

Mrs Richards You know, it has caused quite a lot of problems in our family. I have a little boy, he is eight now. My husband has no time for him at all because he is all Jill now. He very seldom talks to Bill unless it's to tell him off, and Jill, like most mentally retarded children, is very affectionate, very loving, although in the next minute she can be very spiteful. My husband expects Bill to accept all this. Well you can't expect a normal healthy boy of eight to take all this and have his hair pulled. So of course he will give her one back, then my husband will have a go at him, then I have a go at my husband and that's how it goes on.

CLH How do the older ones see it?

Mrs Richards Well, naturally they spoil her as well, but they haven't pushed out Bill either.

CLH Do they make it up to him a bit?

Mrs Richards Well they try, you know. I try to . . . there are some times I feel I could give him one when he is naughty or playing up, but I don't. I think, well, if Dad is always on to him Mum can't be. He has got to feel someone loves him and wants him. So it is creating problems all round. I don't think people realize the problems it creates.

CLH Do your children play with her?

Mrs Richards Oh, Bill plays with her, but he is the next one. . . Oh, yes, you know, she is good fun, she enjoys herself and runs round the table. No, she doesn't worry me, but I worry when the doctors say we might lose her when she is seven, you know, but apart from that, well, she is like a normal child really, you know, in conversation and that.

CLH How would you know that something is the matter?

Sue People say she is a bit blue, isn't she? Across her nose and that, and people can tell like that, but I can't, you know.

I asked my second boy, Simon, to dictate to me what he

thought about David. David was nine years old at the time and Simon was seven-and-a-half. As far as I can tell Simon does not seem in any way deprived or held back because he has a mentally handicapped brother. He realizes that he has some responsibility for David. We sometimes fear that we ask him to do too much but Simon likes his responsibility; 'It is very difficult for Mummy and Daddy because they don't understand him'. I know what he means: we are often intolerant and angry and it may very well seem to him that we don't treat his brother very well. David in some ways is an ideal brother: he is not competitive and everything Simon does is bound to be better. I typed:

Simon My brother is mentally handicapped. It is very difficult to speak to him. I find it rather easy to understand what he is saying. I think that is because I used to sleep in the same room as him. He is nine now and it is very difficult to get him from place to place because he wants to see all the same things all the time, like raindrops: he sits on the pavement watching the drops. His favourite animals are horses, cows and sheep.

David is a very mischievous boy. His usual trick is trying to get the biscuits out of the tin on the shelf; another one is getting into my bed, he also jumps on me and fights. He likes banging on his drum and makes us all go mad. He had a guitar for his birthday and he plays that. It is very difficult for Mummy and Daddy because they don't understand him.

When we go on holiday without him I feel very sad because I miss his snoring which stops me from having bad dreams. There is only one other boy who can cope with him and that is Adam Steele. He is the son of a doctor. David is very fat because he eats lots of bread and butter and biscuits. I have known David longer and I like him a bit better than Toby [younger brother, aged four-and-a-half]. We have some people who help with taking David for walks and help us. They are very nice to David.

Mr and Mrs Davis's boy is eight and he has a sister who is fifteen years older. Having a mentally handicapped child in

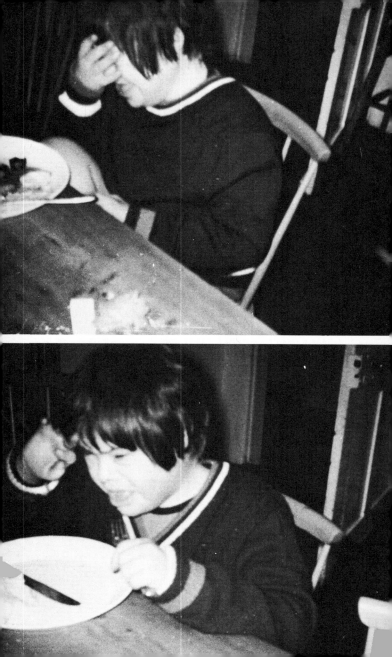

one's family must arouse some fears and there is still enough nonsense talked about 'bad blood' and inherited defects to warrant taking all this seriously and discussing it with a specialist. If the whole matter is ignored these secret fears become harmful.

CLH How old was your daughter when Christopher was born?
Mrs Davis Fifteen.
CLH How did she feel about it? Did she talk about it?
Mrs Davis Well, we didn't tell her, we were advised not to, and this was a big mistake. We did not really discuss it until he was over a year old.
Mr Davis Yes, her friends had said to her that they were sure he was mentally handicapped. I don't think they should ever advise you to keep your family in the dark.
CLH Who is 'they'?
Mrs Davis Oh, the hospital, they said 'don't tell her', you know. He looked quite a normal baby after he got over his severe illness when he was born. My daughter mentioned it to her doctor when she got married, and he said it was very unlikely that she would have a mentally handicapped child and she has a nice intelligent child now. We have talked more about it since she married. One little incident I remember about our daughter: I had to go home and tell her that her new brother was in an incubator and wasn't very well and might not live, and I said 'I am not going to worry you with these problems, just carry on normally and come home and cook me something and get on with your schooling etc.', and she said 'Any problem that's your problem is my problem, because after all he is my brother'.

Mrs Hopkins's mentally handicapped boy is the eldest of three boys. All three were born close together so she really had three babies to look after at the same time. When there is a crisis, like the measles epidemic she describes, the burden is even greater because the family with a handicapped child has 'less to spare': it lives nearer the edge of the volcano and the fear is that everything will just go to pieces.

Mrs Hopkins When the third child was born we had another screaming baby who kept us awake at night and I tended to reject the other two completely because I was so exhausted by feeding and coping with the new baby. I think John [the eldest child, who is a mongol] suffered most from this because by then Richard, the second baby, was nearly three and we could explain to him what was going on, but John still was not talking although he was physically very active . . . When Jason [the third] was born John went into the residential unit and started measles while he was there. He had to go to hospital when Jason was only ten days old.

At the hospital John would not take the food they gave him because it was not the sort of food he was used to . . . I decided that the only thing to do was to spend most of the afternoon there and take food for John myself, and so I did this: feed Jason, take him out in his carry-cot in the back of the car, park him underneath Sister's window, take John his food, give it to him, take his nappies off and try to treat his very sore bottom, play with him and talk to him; while I was there perhaps go back and feed Jason in the car, and then come home and deal with Richard who by then also had measles!

. . . I had to stop going out with three children as it was not safe to leave a pram standing with a toddler sitting on it and a baby inside it while I ran after John.

John's brother says he is miserable if the family goes on holiday without John, but at eight he is old enough to realize the problems of caring for John in a strange house, especially as he knows that John does not like the unfamiliar and would behave even more oddly than he does at home. On the other hand, the family is incomplete without him.

In the case of Mrs Shepherd the mentally handicapped child is the younger of the two and the older one seems 'a little bit frightened'. It may be frightening to see a brother or a sister doing things that are known to be 'naughty'.

This poses a problem for parents. Two systems of justice have to be set up which leave room for manipulation and my children often instigate mischief which David (the handicapped one) carries out very happily.

CLH Do you find that you treat the children differently?
Mrs Shepherd Yes, I think we have to.
Mr Shepherd It does make problems . . . We try to make it up to Joyce to a certain extent. I think she suffers a bit because we have had difficulties in having children to come and play. Other children are a little bit frightened and of course her friends are quite young and Stephen is quite big. Joyce says 'Mummy can we come in ?' and I say 'Yes'; they go and play in a separate room. I don't make them play with Stephen.
CLH Does Joyce imitate him?
Mrs Shepherd No, she doesn't. If anything she tends to worry about it and she will rush around cleaning up after him and looking at me with one eye and hoping that I am not going to be too cross about it. She is very sensitive and I think it tends to make children far too responsible for their age, which is why I am a little easier on her in other ways.

The Peters family consists of two children; Brenda, the older one, aged seven, is made anxious by her sister, and the parents fear they may have neglected her. Parents have to devote their energies to 'keeping going' and the normal children may feel neglected, just because there isn't enough energy to go round. Brenda's parents feel they have so many problems of their own that they have not looked after **her** well enough. However, she has a very understanding teacher in the school who gives her special attention because she knows how difficult things are for the family. Brenda is made very anxious by the 'dreadful' things her sister does and keeps on saying, 'Mummy, look what Mary is doing.' On the other hand, Mrs Williams's eldest boy largely ignores his younger brother except at night when he cannot sleep because of the noise and general chaos that Bobby creates.

CLH Do you get a good night's sleep?
Mrs Williams Well, sometimes he's there, banging on the wall . . . he's not a very good sleeper. He's there banging on the wall or singing. I was going to apply for a three-bedroomed house and I thought, well, if I could get him a room on his own and then put a little — I know it's an awful thing to say — put a little lock or a bolt on his door, to make sure he stays in there, 'cos it's not fair on the other one.
CLH Does he wake the other children?
Mrs Williams Well, Harold's got to sleep in with us, but Glynn sleeps in with him and there's Glynn in there shouting 'Shut up I want to get to sleep!' But the thing is, when they put you in those houses they never want to move you.

In the Jenkins family the mentally handicapped son is between an older sister and a newly-born baby brother. Again the parents seem to be able to take the handicap in their stride and want very much to treat the children as if there were no differences.

Mr Jenkins Peter is not unmanageable and we find that we can treat him the same as his sister. I don't know whether people will take him the same as they take his sister . . . he's no different.
Mrs Jenkins We've never had to try. In fact they make a lot more fuss of him than they do the others really . . . though he can be terrible at times, when you are shopping he loves you to chase him round the shop; on the whole he is well behaved.

Comments and recommendations

1 If the advice is to keep the child in the family it must be seen to be best for all the family, not just the mentally handicapped child. At this point the financial resources and the amount of help available must be considered. If the advice is to put the child into an institution then the potentially frightening effect on brothers and sisters must be taken into account; it may seem to them that a member of the family can just be removed at will, or because he is 'naughty'.

2 Normal children are presented with a number of standards of behaviour, whether in school, church or in the homes of relatives and friends, on which they learn to model themselves. The mentally handicapped child introduces another dimension into the dynamics of the family. Most parents try very hard to improve the quality of the lives their children lead. The pressure the mentally handicapped child exerts on them reduces the possibility of achieving a higher standard or even maintaining a degree of stability.

3 The mentally handicapped child presents a burden that should not be put entirely on any one member of the family, particularly his brothers or sisters. It is important that they are allowed to entertain friends separately, should they wish to do so.

4 Brothers and sisters may be under pressure that is not necessarily apparent to the parents. GPs, teachers and social workers should be alerted to the possibility of stress once they know that there is a mentally handicapped child in the family.

CHAPTER 6
UPBRINGING

We go up the wall sometimes with this
spitting business . . . people will say to you,
you know, that's nothing, but after months
and years of listening to it, it is a lot. He
grinds his teeth

Quite apart from crisis points such as the actual birth and the illnesses, there is the slow grind of bringing up the child. At times it is difficult to distinguish the problems of 'normal' child-rearing from those specifically related to mentally handicapped children. All children get on their parents' nerves, they all make messes and they all need and demand more attention than most adults can normally give them. The difference lies in the expectations: with a normal child the stages of development merge and pass and, however ghastly the mess, one knows that in due course toilet-training will be achieved, speech will come and the usual social skills will be acquired. The mentally handicapped child often moves ahead so slowly that one despairs of ever achieving the next stage. The parents interviewed show that progress, however slow, is possible.

Many of the parents mention the speech problem. Speech is so vital. We structure our experience through speech, learning becomes easier, emotion can be expressed through words, and frustration is reduced correspondingly. When the child is unable to speak, a number of problems arise. Some children at the time of the interview were unable to talk even though the maximum age was eight. However, there were children who were capable of some speech and this helped enormously: the child could make his wishes known and there was correspondingly less frustration.

Mr and Mrs Davis describe very vividly the everyday problems. Like several other parents they dispel the myth that all mongols are affectionate, lovable and cuddly — this may be the case in institutions, where mongols often seem to provide the 'stable' element. They also bring out the problem of annoying habits. As married couples know, we all have habits that can barely be tolerated by the other partner. What makes the 'annoying habit' of the mentally handicapped child worse is that it is a continuous reminder of the handicap; spitting, tooth-grinding or even dangling bits of string hark back to the early disappointments, and accentuate other difficulties such as lack of sleep and the fear that the child may run away or do some extensive mischief.

Skills which other children develop naturally are not denied to mentally handicapped children. With encouragement, creative ability can be expressed in a variety of ways

Mrs Davis They say mongols settle down very well and are very happy, but Christopher isn't, he is a very withdrawn child . . . he likes to be among people, but he doesn't like anyone to approach him — and he likes, for want of a better expression, proper things rather than toys; he likes real motor-cars, he won't play with a toy motor-car.

Mr Davis He doesn't see as much as other children.

Mrs Davis You see, if you cuddle him he pushes you away, but he stills wants your attention, so it is not easy to have a relationship with him.

Mr Davis You mustn't force him to do anything, you must persuade him; I have never tried to the point of hurting, but a slap on his backside, if he is naughty, is in his view a bit of a joke, so there is no point in pursuing the matter. You have just got to try and explain what you are trying to do.

Mrs Davis You have more impression on him than I have because my voice doesn't impress him: his father's voice if he is annoyed is far more effective than mine.

CLH What sort of things does he do?

Mr Davis Nothing frightful; he has this habit of lying on his tummy at home and just rocking and perhaps doing a little spitting out of his mouth, more or less makes a tune like pppppppp, this sort of business, and we want him to sit properly and be active, because if he lies around, particularly at weekends, he is apt not to have a full night's sleep and we suffer.

Mrs Davis He plays the record-player; he can do it all now except unlatch the lid and lift it up when the record's ended. The other difficulty we have, of course, and I haven't mentioned it so far, is that he can't talk at all and therefore communication is really very difficult for anyone coming to the house because they can't really converse with him at all.

CLH When he does not get his way does he have tantrums?

Mrs Davis He has tantrums at the training centre because they make him do things, which is quite right. He needs discipline and he does not get it at home; I get it if I insist on him dressing himself; he raises Cain and I can't stand it so I give him a hand, which is wrong, I shouldn't do it.

CLH Does he tap or bang?
Mrs Davis Flicks.
Mr Davis Forefinger and thumb.
Mrs Davis The spoon, he is a dangler.
Mr Davis He is a dangler all right . . . we take all pieces of string and anything like that away from him immediately.
Mrs Davis I don't know if that is any good either really, but still . . . .
Mr Davis He will still do it if he gets hold of anything that will in fact dangle, he just likes to see it, to and fro like a pendulum . . . We go up the wall sometimes with this spitting business . . . and what is more people will say to you, 'Well, you know, that's nothing', but after months and years of listening to it, it is a lot. He grinds his teeth.
Mrs Davis Within the house he is getting fed up with his record-player; now we can't find out what he would like to do next.
Mr Davis He won't watch TV.
Mrs Davis He won't look at a book.
Mr Davis He likes being taken out . . . he likes perhaps going to a playground, but there again he will leave your hand and dash at the swing even if somebody is swinging there. One day he is going to get his face split open. Now that we are fifty we can't catch him up and this is terrifying. He was missing from home once, because he can open doors now, and my wife rang me up at work and said 'Christopher is missing'. I am in the middle of a meeting. I collected two of my staff and said 'We have to dash off home to do a search for Christopher', and by the time we had got there he had turned up again.

One of the additional worries is that most mentally handicapped children have little or no sense of danger. They cannot anticipate it. Often they cannot say clearly who they are. If the child looks normal this makes matters even worse. If the child needs constant supervision but still escapes, like Mrs Williams the mother may be told that she is not looking after the child properly.

Mrs Williams Before he used to run out into the road anywhere.

CLH Has he got no sense of danger?

Mrs Williams No. He'd . . . climb anywhere. One day he was missing and was gone for two hours, we had the police out looking for him. They found him over at Blackmoor — sat in the middle of the road, he wouldn't move. But the policeman said someone must have seen him cross the busy roads. The times I've looked out there and seen buses stop and Bobby's just been standing in the road. And I pleaded with them, it was to do with this health visitor that came here, to get somebody to fence off the garden for me. Now they told me, if I bought the wood, they'd get the council to do it. I couldn't afford it! I mean, it would have cost the earth to have it up all around the back — 'cos that's all open and this is where he used to get out. Well then he got into the habit of just diving over the hedge and then he'd be out there where the buses stop. Talk about a cat with nine lives, I think he's had a hundred lives. The times he's been out on that road — and then somebody tells me I ought to look after him.

The description Mrs Shepherd gives of bringing up her mentally handicapped child seems fairly typical. It certainly corresponds quite closely to my own experience. Messy incidents before toilet-training is achieved really are upsetting, and one does not have to be 'anal fixated' to mind very much if there is excrement all over the place. Mrs Shepherd resorts to smacking and feels guilty afterwards. Then there is the conflict between allowing the child to do as much as possible for himself, or doing things for him because one is in a hurry. Here the school can achieve much; the pattern of 'Mummy do it' has not been established and the cool expectation that the child can do things for himself seems to produce results. This is why it is important to get the child to school early so that the right patterns can be impressed on his mind. Once the wrong ones are there, it is extremely difficult to alter them.

Mrs Shepherd He is eight and we have to dress him . . . and he still wears nappies at night . . . .

Mr Shepherd We get on quite well, you couldn't possibly not get on with him, but it is more of an effort on your part to make him do things, to make him get up and walk around and go and play or sing. You have got to do things with him, otherwise he tends not to do much on his own.

Mrs Shepherd The thing is Stephen would come in and perhaps sit down for a couple of hours and do practically nothing, and then he would go on what we call a rampage round the house. He has definite things in each room that he does, especially in the kitchen — it is a sort of organized trip, but we are slowly managing to get a few things back on the shelf.

He still wears nappies at night but he is pretty good during the day. He has no speech at all . . . not a single word, not persistently, you know. The other morning I was getting him dressed and he came in and said 'clothes', as clearly as anything, but he has never said it since, and you can't get him to say it again.

Mrs Shepherd You know, when we get these awful accidents, when he has lost his pants here, and I am not around and he takes them off, it means scrubbing everything practically from top to bottom and you just don't know where to start . . . .

Mr Shepherd We have tried, I think this is where the strain comes in really, you need one eye on him all the time, you know.

Mrs Shepherd How do we control him? We try but it does not seem to work although they have said at school recently that he does get a bit more upset and he cries if they are really displeased, so this may be a sign of emotional development, but in the end if I take recourse to smacks I find that I feel very guilty afterwards. Actually I feel sometimes that one gets so tense that one does smack too hard.

To parents who have been deeply influenced by Spock and Winnicott, Mr Peters's account given on p. 80, of disciplining his child must make painful reading. Among middle-class parents, particularly, there is much emphasis on reasoning with the child. Instead of physical threat, speech is used as a weapon to bring normal children to order. The chaotic behaviour of the mentally handicapped infant brings out some of the fears many of us have about controlling children. Many times one feels that all discipline will break down if one does not 'draw a line somewhere'. With mentally handicapped children the lines of demarcation are less distinct and often the child will frighten one by his behaviour. With our own child we are frequently much more authoritarian than we would like to be and this is of course noticed by the other children. Our lack of consistency worries them at times and this must add to their sense of insecurity.

Mr and Mrs Peters's daughter, Mary, is four. Mr Peters felt that he must be the firm one out of the two parents; that he must be the one to train the child to behave and to be disciplined. After a time he found this difficult because he could see the fear in Mary's eyes, like when he was training dogs (he is very fond of dogs and understands them). He felt he was treating the child too harshly and yet he could not help himself because he knew that his wife was desperate. His physical pain was always with him (from an industrial accident) and the banging, rocking and screaming of the child became too much for him. Their sleep was constantly interrupted because Mary would come into their bed at all hours. In the end he slept nearest to the door so that when Mary tried to get in he could take her back into her bed. He has been very strict and it hurts him when the child insists on going to her mother rather than to him.

In the house Mary is very difficult; she spills things, such as a whole packet of Vim, all over the place; the wall in the lounge had to be painted again because of the scribblings on the wall. Sometimes Mary runs into the street and then people who don't know about the brain damage blame the parents as if they had been negligent.

The problem of looking after the child and preventing him from running away is illustrated by Mrs Hopkins. When the child does run off for a long time the police may have to be called. The parents will feel guilty at having caused so much fuss and bother; and there is the fear of accidents to himself or to others, or that he might lock himself in a car boot for instance. There is very little appreciation of danger or anticipation of difficulty in a mentally handicapped child and although one may know this rationally it is still not easy to anticipate each crisis, particularly if one wants the child to gain some independence. There remains the fear of spoiling the child, or of not sensing when he really needs help or when he is 'having everyone on'.

Mrs Hopkins's boy is capable of learning things. This is important and perhaps may show parents with younger children who are feeling depressed that there is progress, but this is hard to notice. Occasionally we say to each other 'he couldn't (or wouldn't) have done that last year'.

Mrs Hopkins When he was a baby he took hours to feed and he couldn't burp without bringing up food, getting him on to solids was murder, but we did eventually. Now we can't stop him eating . . . we had masses of advice on toilet-training but of course we didn't even attempt to toilet-train him for a long time and he wasn't clean and dry until his younger brother was clean and dry which must have been not until he was five. He was dry during the day-time except for occasional accidents, but he was still in nappies at night until he was almost five and he has continued to have accidents during the day and at night, but not quite so much at night as during the day until he was about seven. Now at the age of eight he takes himself to the toilet and he has very few unintended accidents.

If the parents of mentally handicapped children want them to make good progress, they must be prepared to devote themselves wholeheartedly to the task. When a living has to be earned and there are other children to be cared for, this is a tremendous task.

Mrs Hopkins Unless you happen to catch John at the moment when he is willing to learn he'll just get up and walk off or try to do something else. In order to try and teach him anything

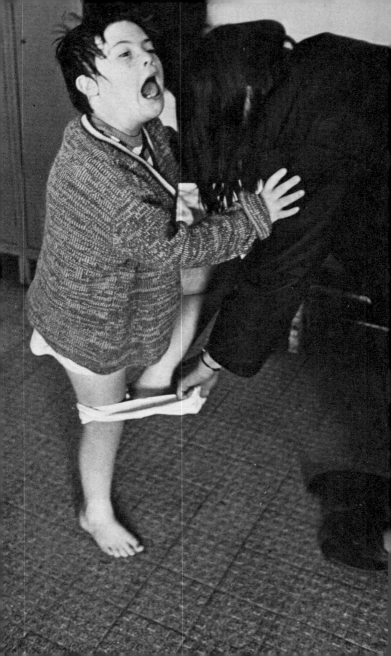

There are everyday things the child can do for himself, but he will need help with many others

at all and to get him to cooperate you have to càtch him in the right mood, often then you can teach him quite a lot. He's learnt a lot of little songs and his words were coming along quite nicely, and he can help tidy up and make a bed if he feels like it; if not, of course, he can turn the whole place upside down, pee all over the floor and things.

When John was very young we used to spend a lot of time exercising him and letting him pull himself up with his hands and he made very fast progress until he was about a year old . . . his speech has been very, very slow. He had the odd sound at the usual time of about twelve to fifteen months, but it was not until he was quite old, about three, that he started to say one or two words. Now at the age of eight he has quite a good vocabulary and communicates quite well. This is one of the most difficult things to deal with because you can't leave him with strangers who are unable to communicate with him. It makes him very difficult if he can't communicate and he gets very, very cross and frustrated.

Holidays present a special problem. At home one can make some provision for dealing with an over-active child and be on guard against his tricks. On holiday everything is strange and exciting and for the parents it can be a nightmare rather than a holiday.

Mrs Hopkins The holiday was a great strain, particularly as John developed a tendency to run away at about the age of six. He was fairly easy to control when he was small as he couldn't get up the speed to run away but as he grew older and faster and I already had perhaps a baby in a pram and a toddler to look after, I found it more and more difficult to go out with the three children . . . Now he has discovered that he can open the front door by himself. We have fixed a chain but even so he gets a chair and gets at the chain . . . we are hoping that as he gets older he won't run away quite so much, I think he only wants to go out because he is bored.

This is one of the greatest of our problems: what to do with him at the weekends and during the holidays. He gets

extremely bored . . . I find that except for one or two friends
people will say 'Oh, yes, he went that way' but they wouldn't
dream of stopping him. They just watch him go. He has been
brought back, but on the whole people just tend to note that
he has gone past and do nothing about it. He ran off to the
zoo on one occasion and he must have looked very odd as he
was wearing his little brother's shirt, stomach sticking out and
a great gap in the middle. But apparently no one noticed him
at the zoo or took him under control.

Mr and Mrs Jenkins seem to have less of a problem because
Peter is a high-grade mongol, but it does show what a wide
range of ability there is among mentally handicapped children.
It is amusing to note that at the centre he is regarded as 'a
feather in their cap'. The parents clearly are very keen to have
him learn to read and write and their hopes may be realistic.
With other parents it may be necessary to help them
understand the limited aptitudes of their child. Sometimes it
may be more important to develop other skills or to develop a
system of priorities.

Mrs Jenkins We treat Peter as a normal child. We know that he
does things slower, but we still expect him to do things and he
does them. We can take him out anywhere, but there again we
were lucky, we have a high-grade mongol and usually he is
pretty good, but if he decides he doesn't want to do something
he won't . . . .
Mr Jenkins Small things sometimes, he might not want to eat
his dinner. You say 'Come on now, eat those potatoes' and
he'll say he doesn't like potatoes and you know he damn well
loves potatoes, he can never eat enough of them, but he's just
got that funny thing into his head that he won't eat them and
he won't. We can let him out and leave him out there. We have
told him enough times 'You can't go past the end of that road'
and he will stay out there quite happy.
Mrs Jenkins He writes his name, and he can write Mummy and
Daddy, and Rose. There's even talk now of getting him to an
ESN school . . . but the education authorities are holding it up,

and at the centre they want him to go because it would be a feather in their cap, wouldn't it?

Mr Jenkins They say he might go for twelve months, but this has been going on since Christmas; the educational people are dragging their feet over it, but we shall be very pleased if he does because I think he could learn to read and write if he was pushed.

While the mentally handicapped child is at the chaotic stage, neither toilet-trained nor able to communicate verbally, either over-active or too passive, the rest of the family will be going through their worst time. It must depend a great deal upon where the family lives and how well-off it is. A child banging monotonously for more than half an hour at a time must cause resentment among neighbours if the family live in a flat; in any case the parents will feel self-conscious and guilty.

There is a great need for vastly increased nursery education for all children in this country. For mentally handicapped children the need is even more urgent and the fact that the pre-school period may be the worst for the parents should be noted by local authorities and social agencies. Although, on the whole, good provision is made in many areas for the child over five, in many cases very little is done for the infants.

Comments and recommendations

1 Opportunities for mothers to talk to each other in the presence of either doctors or social workers were found to be particularly helpful. Since all the mothers present have children with mental handicaps, no one can seem to have an advantage or could possibly be seen to be claiming some sort of superiority. It helps to know that there are others who are worse off, and one may pick up some useful advice. Doctors and social workers need to learn by direct experience how the problems are seen by members of the group. Group meetings save time and may prepare the ground for individual contact.

2 Nursery playgroups and nursery schools are urgently needed. Early stimulation is vital, time-consuming and often impossible for parents with other children. Nursery groups where mothers help will also provide a meeting-place for those with similar problems and a chance for mixing normal and handicapped children.

3 There are some good records which help with speech and movement; they may also stimulate interest as well as give some pleasure.

Remember that the development of the mentally handicapped child is slower than that of the normal child, so that the age quoted in books for various activities may not be the appropriate one (see p. 124).

4 Other children should be encouraged to play with the handicapped child. They should be told what is the matter with the child and what he can and cannot do.

5 The over-active child may need tranquillizers at night, which in turn will give the rest of the family a good night's sleep and make the child more manageable during the day. Activities such as swimming or visits to an adventure playground will stimulate the inert child and provide activity for the over-active child.

CHAPTER 7
THE NEXT CHILD

The only drawback was that six months passed before they actually fitted us in and by that time I was five months pregnant; and also the tests take five weeks and we were waiting for the results. They came two months after the second child was born

Many mothers find it hard to believe that they can produce a perfect child and there are often fears before birth that something may be wrong with the baby. It is quite shattering when these fears are actually confirmed, and even more so when the first child happens to be mentally handicapped and the parents are young and want more children. Laplace, a French mathematician, seemed undisturbed by the bombardments during the siege of Paris in 1871 and when asked why he was so calm, replied that he walked under the cover of the law of probability. This kind of calm will disappear when disaster, however unlikely it may have seemed before, has actually struck.

Mr and Mrs Shepherd received genetic counselling, but since the results of the test only came up two months after the second child was born most of the benefits were lost. Mrs Shepherd's distrust of doctors is significant, as also is the great strain; something of which she was not aware at the time.

CLH How did you hear about the genetic counselling scheme?
Mrs Shepherd Do you know, honestly I can't think, we must have heard of it somewhere. We asked the doctor and he wrote off . . . people, medical people, said, 'You ought to have another baby, it couldn't happen another time'. Occasionally it does and I do feel they made a mistake over this because someone we know had a second handicapped baby and I have wondered many times what happens if someone has two mongols. . . . When we came to have the tests they were extremely helpful, they did a very extensive test . . . blood tests, matching up the colour of your eyes and all sorts of things. They were extremely pleasant. . . . The only drawback was that six months passed before they actually fitted us in and by that time I was five months pregnant; and also the tests take five weeks and we were waiting for the results. They came two months after he [the second child] was born. So actually it was a period of stress for me, the latter part of my pregnancy, because they said the results would be in six weeks and they ended up by taking five months, and of course I was beginning to wonder if everyone was happy with the results . . .

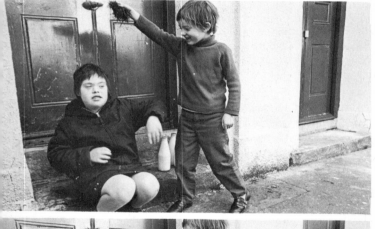

I have a great distrust of doctors now; I am afraid because they hoodwinked us so much over Stephen. I found once or twice when he was small and had tonsilitis, I automatically wondered whether there was anything wrong with his heart. The doctor came and examined him and I would watch him like a hawk because the only way to get the truth is to watch his face and even then doctors manage to look impassive, don't they? But I have this distrust of doctors and really I don't believe a word they say.

CLH Waiting for the second child was a strain?

Mrs Shepherd I didn't appear the least bit worried. I didn't realize that I felt worried, but I must have I think, because I had high blood pressure which wasn't toxaemia, it was a nervous thing, and I ended up by having to stay in hospital.

Mr Shepherd I don't think it showed too much but I was a bit worried, you know, because we still weren't sure and my wife was in and out of hospital like a yo-yo . . . a couple of weeks in, a couple of weeks out and then she had to go in three weeks before the birth, quite some time . . . my big problem was, you know, what am I going to do with Stephen. Again the authorities could come up with no help at all.

The physical handicap which occurred with Mrs Hopkins's second child was very hard to bear. In a way she seemed to suffer more that time because the event reactivated all the feelings that had come with the birth of the first, mentally handicapped, boy. Considered dispassionately, the defect was not only slight but soon cured; the difficulties at the time, however, were felt to be great and were probably not recognized because to all intents and purposes the baby was normal and very healthy.

Mrs Hopkins After we had genetic tests we had to make up our minds about having another baby and everybody said since the mongolism was of the erratic type there should be no danger whatsoever of the next child being a mongol. So we did decide to go ahead and have another baby. In a way, when the second child was born with a physical handicap, he had a bilateral dislocation of both hips, this was an even worse blow than John's mental handicap. (He was perfectly all right after eleven

weeks in a metal frame, by the way.) I found that we were
both very tense while I was pregnant with the second baby,
and this, perhaps combined with the fact that he had a defect,
made me resent the second baby and this may have made him
difficult to deal with. He was a screaming baby who stayed
awake at night and wanted constant feeding, cuddling and
handling and this meant that John had a rather raw deal as
obviously one's duty is towards the new baby.

Mrs Jenkins talks about her fear 'because I had one normal
one, and one handicapped one, and I thought, well, it's more
likely that I'll have another abnormal one now, you know'.
When the last child was born it seemed ages to her before she
was told that it was normal. To overworked doctors and nurses
a couple of days may not seem a long time; for Mrs Jenkins it
was an eternity before she knew that her new child was all
right. When there has been a handicapped child in the family it
might be a good idea to reassure the parents very quickly
indeed, if this is possible. The waiting period will have been
much harder for them to bear, and they may be considerably
more tense than other parents.

CLH . . . and two years after you'd had the mentally
handicapped one you decided to have the next child. Did you
take any advice on this?
Mrs Jenkins Well, the doctor just said, 'If I were you, I would
have another baby, right away.'
CLH Was it a rough time waiting?
Mr Jenkins Yes, it was.
Mrs Jenkins Very much so.
Mr Jenkins I can say it now. I think mentally she had a worse
time with Beatrice, who is two years younger than Peter, than
she did with the oldest.
Mrs Jenkins We never bothered with counselling. No one
suggested anything, so we didn't do anything.
CLH Did you go and see that gynaecologist?
Mrs Jenkins We saw a doctor, but he didn't suggest any tests or
anything.

Mr Jenkins No, he just told us to go ahead with it; all they did was to take blood tests of Peter . . . .

CLH You said you were suffering, were you anxious?

Mrs Jenkins Yes, I used to get awfully upset, crying, wondering what was going to happen. I was almost afraid when I had her, to ask. In fact I didn't ask, I waited for them to say that she was perfectly all right.

CLH Were they quick to tell you?

Mrs Jenkins Well, they didn't tell me right away, not even then. The consultant came round one day and said I had a mongol child and said that this one was perfectly all right, and that was the first I had heard. I had been afraid to ask.

CLH How long after the birth was that?

Mrs Jenkins Only a few days because I was only in there for four days — it was probably a couple of days, that was all. If I had asked they probably would have told me. They should have told me earlier.

It would seem that Mr and Mrs Peters badly needed the help of a geneticist, as well as information: what were the sort of defects of the two mentally handicapped children of someone Mr Peters had heard of? Were these in any way like those of his child? Could one separate out the rational fears from the irrational? Mr Peters was certain that they would not have any more children: 'Once I make my mind up that's it.' Mrs Peters was less certain and seemed sad about the decision, but what really frightened them was the nine months' wait and the fear that it could happen again. When deciding whether to have another child, genetic advice should be made available (perhaps more speedily than in the case of Mr and Mrs Shepherd) but it is not enough by itself; there must be explanation and counselling. What seems straightforward to an expert on genetics may not be so obvious to a non-scientist. Added to this there is the nine-month waiting period, which will seem to be a very long time for the parents. When there is another genetic defect, as in Mrs Hopkins's case, the distress will be very great because all the old feelings will come up again. In families where there is stability, confidence and mutual support these are stresses that will be overcome.

Although it was never discussed in the interviews one may assume that in some instances the birth of a mentally handicapped child will make for sexual difficulties between husband and wife. Neither the fear of pregnancy nor all the depression and distress can be conducive to a happy sex life.

The worst thing is the period of waiting for the next child: all the couples who went ahead and had another child mentioned this. We found it very reassuring to be told immediately that our last child was not a mongol or abnormal in any way; even two days waiting seemed too long to Mrs Jenkins.

Comments and recommendations

1 Birth control must be used from the moment the couple resume sexual relations. Therefore advice on contraceptives and family planning is essential as soon as possible after birth. With many doctors and clinics this is standard practice, but it cannot be taken for granted. After the birth of the mentally handicapped child there may well be fears of conception and therefore an increase in general tension. Good advice on contraception may lessen this tension.

If information on birth control is not readily available locally ring the Family Planning Association (see p. 126) and they will tell you where you can find help in your part of the country. The Brook Advisory Clinic will do the same. Ring their London Head Office (see p. 126).

2 The most common fear is that the next child will also be abnormal. The best way of allaying this fear is to have genetic counselling, and for this to be useful it must be given **before** the next pregnancy. Not all parents will know about this sort of advice, which we certainly found to be invaluable. Hospitals, doctors, midwives and health visitors should be provided with information about the availability of genetic counselling.

Your doctor should be able to tell you where the nearest centre for genetic counselling is, and give you a letter to take to the centre. Should you be unable to obtain this information from your doctor, write to the Social Services Department at MIND (see p. 126).

3 Parents should be told **immediately** after the birth of the next child whether or not there is any degree of handicap, or whether this is suspected.

CHAPTER 8
TRAINING CENTRES AND OTHER OUTSIDE HELP

So I got on to the Social Services and all they said to me was 'You feel better now we've talked' and I thought to meself, 'well, that was a waste of two pence'

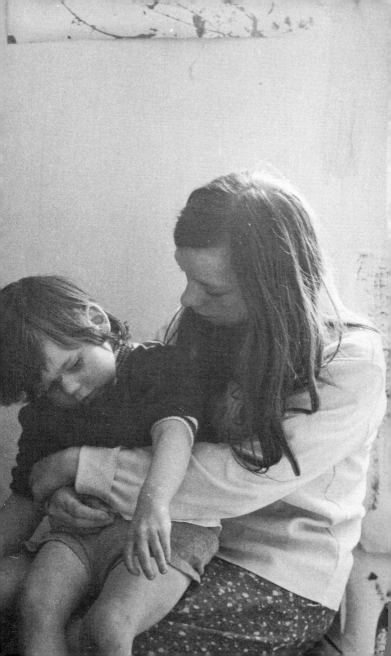

The amount of help that parents receive from outside the home varies tremendously. It emerged fairly clearly from the interviews I had, that the more educated and articulate the parents were, the more likely they were to get help in the form of playgroups and so on. Where provisions are scarce or inadequate, it seems that those parents who stand up and claim their rights are the ones who get most help and support. The parents I talked to were relatively self-reliant and competent people and yet a frequent statement is summed up by 'whatever help we have had, we have had to fight for'. The harder help is to come by, the more difficult and 'fight-minded' the parents will become. In the end these parents will get less, and may become isolated, because the authorities in turn become suspicious and defensive.

The three working-class families I interviewed certainly had a worse time of it than the other parents. It would be rash on the basis of three interviews to generalize about the availability of provisions, but there is a good deal of evidence elsewhere that even the benefits the Welfare State offers are not taken up sufficiently by working-class people. Sometimes the authorities seem to conserve scarce resources, instead of saying to their clients 'This, this and this is what you are entitled to'. No one had ever come to the parents with a check-list (if indeed it had ever existed) and said to them 'Get what you can, you need it'. For example: a year after payments of the Attendance Allowance have started, Mrs Williams has only just heard about it from her niece.

There is a great deal of evidence of help that was given readily and kindly, and some could be described as 'exceeding the call of ordinary duty'. But in the experience of our own family, although we can say that we have been helped a great deal, the initiative has always come from us. When David was nearly driving us to despair because of his unceasing activity we asked for an interview with a consultant who prescribed a tranquillizer and added the splendid message: 'It does not matter whether he takes it or you, it's quite harmless'. In fact the provision of the tranquillizer was a turning point: we had better nights because the child slept, therefore we were better at handling him and he responded by being less anarchic. Why had not one of the agencies that helped us mentioned tranquillizers before?

The enormous benefits of the training centre emerge clearly. They are essential for the handicapped child. Without the help of the teachers the children would make less progress (although Mrs Mercer is not as positive as the other parents on that point). Surely the school and the parents must aim at approaching the problem of education jointly rather than separately. There are difficulties in communication that are entirely understandable: the distance of the school from many homes, the fact that the children can't talk and that the staff are engaged in working with particularly demanding children. But more consultation and some joint approach to the whole problem would help parents and inevitably also the teachers. The parents interviewed here feel exhausted and often discouraged. Surely greater involvement would give them the feeling that they can play a part? Two parents mention a course of speech therapy that was really appreciated. Swimming in the school pool (if there is one) helps because the child **can** swim with water-wings and this sense of achievement is carried over into other activities. In all schools, parental involvement has been proved to be useful. Before long this involvement must include representation on the board of governors. I cannot see how long-term decisions are made by people who have no direct acquaintance with the problems of having mentally handicapped children. Being asked what one really needs is more desirable than an authority deciding what is good for the parents and then being surprised and hurt if the parents want something different.

Once Mrs Williams had got her son into a school for educationally subnormal children, improvement was tremendous.

Mrs Williams This particular health visitor that we had kept promising that Bobby was going to school after Christmas. This was in 1969. Everything was all arranged. Christmas come, but no letter to say Bobby was starting school. This is what I was palmed off with all the time, but then we had

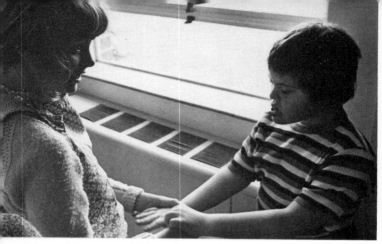

At a training centre children with completely different mental handicaps will be brought together. When the handicap is not immediately obvious it is possibly even more difficult for the parents to cope

another health visitor and she's very nice but she doesn't come here any more, for what reason I don't know but this was the one that tried to get Bobby on holiday last year. She has stopped coming to the house now . . . it's really the teachers now at the school who are more interested in him now, and the psychologist over there.

CLH Are you pleased with the school?

Mrs Williams Oh yes, I reckon it's marvellous. Well, what they've done for Bobby over there, considering he was an absolute little terror when he started.

Mrs Jenkins (talking about Peter's admission to a training centre when he was three-and-a-half) Well the health visitor kept on at me to go and see the headmistress and I sort of put it off and put it off, I didn't want to go. I don't know why. Well in the end she said 'I'll come and take you down' and after that it was all right. I didn't know what to expect and I suppose the longer I kept him away, well, I could imagine to myself that he was normal, but I knew he wasn't. Once he did go he was ever so happy and he loved it, it was better for him.

Mr Jenkins It was a small place. We knew all the teachers personally. My wife said hello to the headmistress every morning and you felt part of the school. We met quite a lot, we had quite a lot of functions and everybody used to help, it was much easier to get involved because everybody felt, you got the impression, that they wanted you to.

CLH What helped and what did not?

Mrs Mercer Well, we had a health visitor but quite frankly she wasn't much help. The first thing she said was, 'My dear, if the baby had to be born somewhere it was a good thing he was born into this family' which wasn't a great help and that's about the only thing she said. Anyway we are very grateful for going to the doctor, we talked about anything you liked. I think looking back on it, it was simply the fact that you thought that somebody was interested in you and the baby. You know, you forget to ask something, and you think 'I will ask that next time I go', and I have talked to other parents who haven't had this, and you know, the child could be three before they know there are any special facilities for caring for them at all.

So I think we were rather lucky that way. She put us in touch with the National Society for Mentally Handicapped Children, and I think I joined when Philip was only two months old and she told us all about the training centre, the workshop and everything. At that time I was convinced he would never sit up, he would never do anything. I thought I was going to feed a vegetable for the rest of my life. Dr Smith told us of many mongol children she had known, and she talked about it — I think she let us talk more than tell us things; you talk about your fears, and of course you see every time we went, she would open her book and say 'Let me see, a month ago he was doing this and that, now he is doing something else'. It made you realize that he **was** making progress. Now Philip goes to school.

CLH Do you feel you have been involved enough in the operation?

Mrs Mercer No, I don't. I was very pleased when they did that speech course last year which we went to, and over a year we have at least got him to repeat words with us; at least he is learning to use words. I think you feel that you are useless, that you are helpless, not being able to help him. I would like to help him. I would like to see more junior training centres, actually, so that we weren't all shoved down there (about eight miles away) because it is impossible to get to the school easily. Lack of transport stops me from going. I went once to join in the swimming. I think it started about 2 p.m. I know I had to leave here at 12.30 . . . and I didn't get back until 4 o'clock. Well, I just can't do it.

Several points made by Mrs Mercer should be stressed. In the first place she had the support of a doctor who took an exceptional interest in parents with mongol children. She was able to talk to her about 'anything you liked' — it takes time to absorb information especially when one is anxious.

When the number of possible consultations is limited there is always the fear that one has forgotten something and many questions are thought of after the interview is over. The interviewer may be very conscientious and say 'Have you any further questions?' but even that implies that time is running a bit short.

Middle-class people are much more competent in this sort of situation; they may even bring a check-list and work through it. What those in authority must realize is that if they really want to help the client he must be allowed to talk in his own way. Just a cheery 'no problems this week?' will produce a good turnover of clients but may not be much use to the individual.

Mrs Mercer did not have much help when she formed the playgroup. Local authorities will often conceal the names of parents with mentally handicapped children, which I am sure is wrong and out-of-date. It underlines that something is wrong and needs to be felt guilty about, and prevents one of the things parents most appreciate: the opportunity to meet others with similar problems, to realize that they are not alone and that there is, in many cases, some progress and hope. This is the valuable function that the NSMHC performs, but if they are not given the names to make an approach some parents may be isolated for too long. Of course there must be an opportunity for anonymity, and medical ethics complicate the issue, but a distinction must be made between discretion and mystification for its own sake. Mrs Mercer could only point out the need by forming a playgroup, but this should be done officially and with all possible speed as a right rather than on the initiative of one rather exceptional mother.

Mrs Hopkins is also for the most part enthusiastic about school.

Mrs Hopkins We first heard about the training centre through the clinic and we were actually told by a neighbour that it might be that they would take our child who was then three-and-a-half. Apparently the clinic at that time did not know that they took very young children and thought that they only went at five, but I understand that the clinics have been brought up-to-date on this. However, if a neighbour hadn't happened to mention this to us we would perhaps not have realized that John could go to the centre quite so early.

So we got him to the training centre when he was three years
and nine months. It was one of the reasons why we couldn't
undertake the conception of the third child . . . We couldn't
find a playgroup for John. I think it was before Mrs Mercer
was running hers for mentally handicapped children. I was at
first pregnant and then had a new baby to look after and so I
wasn't able to undertake much in that line either, so we were
very grateful to the principal of the training centre when she
said she would have John. But it would have been lovely if we
could have formed some sort of playgroup earlier on for him
to run around in.

Five is the normal age for admission to a training centre,
though clearly exceptions have been made to this and the help
was deeply appreciated. For whatever reason, some parents
fared worse than others and the Richards and Peters families
are less enthusiastic about the support they have received than
the Hopkins and Mercer families. As the Shepherds show, the
authorities can be forced to make statutory provisions but
these can be pretty poor. I cannot imagine what good a
twenty-two-mile bus ride did their child.

CLH Did you ask for admission to a training centre?
Mrs Shepherd Yes, I did actually, and they fobbed us off
rather. They said he is making such good progress at home and
you are obviously supplying all the right toys, which we were
actually, so there is really no need for him to go.
Mr Shepherd We had a bit of difficulty in getting him in at
five, yes, we had to push and press and that sort of thing. But I
think that was because we were in — shire; well their excuse
was that they hadn't any room. We said well, he is five now,
you have got to provide something. We had to send him on a
journey of twenty-two miles every day, there and back again.
Mrs Shepherd It used to take about two hours, didn't it?
Mr Shepherd Two hours there and two hours back, but we felt
that we had made our stand; that was all they had to offer and
we had to accept it, didn't we?
Mrs Shepherd Nobody ever backed us in anything.

Mr Shepherd No, not there; we found things much better here. Compared with what we had before we find the training centre here very good and I like the teachers. I know they are very young, but I like the happy atmosphere there and I like the meetings they have there — the ones when you go down to discuss things. Actually I think it would be nice if we did that more often. But there again, if I found I wanted to pop down and collect him I felt quite free and welcome.

Mr Peters feels strongly that what help they have had, they have had to fight for. He has been able to get Mary into a special care unit for two days a week, but the parents think that this is too short to start any adequate training programme and in any case Mr Peters feels that this sort of help is only for a special 'clique' and not their sort. In a way he knows that this is not the case, but says that he begins to believe this when he has to argue about his rights all the time.

Mrs Peters had difficulty in getting Mary into a playgroup. The first help she got was when she heard Mrs Mercer's playgroup had been formed, and saw a feature on television. She finds the playgroup a help because there are other mothers with similar problems.

Mrs Davis Whenever I asked for help the doctor gave it immediately. When Christopher was three he got him into the training centre. A friend told me about it.
CLH Did any official tell you?
Mrs Davis No, because he was under five and they don't take them under five really, so I was worried because to all intents and purposes he was an only child, and he had nobody to play with and he wouldn't mix with other children. I thought if he could be with other children it would be good for him.

Mrs Davis heard about the training centre from a friend, and got Christopher in via the doctor.

Mrs Richards, however, has had no help from official sources with regard to schooling.

Mrs Richards Jill is at home. There is nothing for her whatsoever. The only time she sees other children is Monday afternoons in the playgroup.

CLH How did you hear about that?

Mrs Richards Mrs Mercer advertises; and that's all she gets — two hours on Monday afternoon where she mixes with other children.

CLH How often does the health visitor come?

Mrs Richards She comes quite often from the clinic and is very nice. In fact she has been marvellous these last couple of weeks. She has got on to them about Jill and no one else seems to have bothered about her at all. They put her into the hospital last year into a ward with twenty other children who couldn't speak at all. We discharged her after three days because I didn't think they could get a true assessment of her, not under those conditions because she couldn't converse with any of the children. She ate with a knife and fork when she went in, when she came out she couldn't use them. The doctor was sympathetic but he still thought she would need a month in, but I don't know any other children who have been put in for a month. I have been trying since the beginning of September to find out what school she is going to after Christmas. After all if she was normal and I didn't put her name down I would be in trouble. Right? She is five now, she is due to be educated in some way and I have been trying since September but have got nowhere. I have had the health visitor on to the education officer . . . they always seem to pass you on to someone else and you get through to him and he doesn't know anything about it, so he passes you to somebody else and that's how it goes on, in a vicious circle. When you reach the end of your tether what help might you expect from the Social Services Department?

Mrs Williams I got on to the Social Services, I was crying me eyes out and I explained to them about what Bobby was doing — someone down the road had accused him of damaging his car — and they were more or less trying to put the blame on me, 'cos I was so upset, 'cos my husband was out of work. And she said to me 'Have you any money problems?' and I said 'Well, no, we've got no money problems'. I said 'It's just Bobby is my

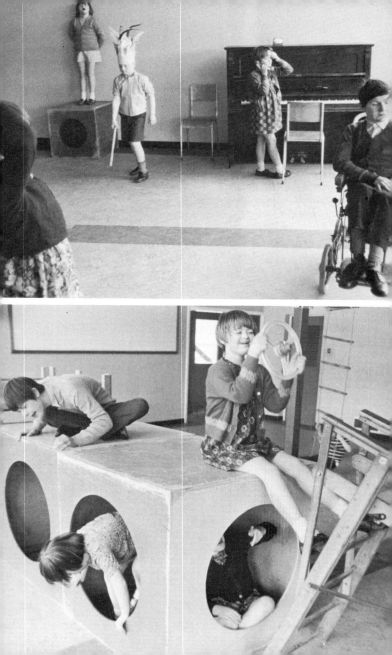

problem'. So I said 'He just will not leave the van alone'. I said 'And the man has been out, shouting at me, telling me about a twenty pound bill he'd be sending me if he does any damage'. So anyway I stopped crying, so she said to me 'You feel better now you've explained it and got it off your chest'. And that was the end of that. It was a waste of two pence.

Mr Davis also feels that arrangements are made for him which he has not asked for or been consulted on and so are unsatisfactory.

You see I wouldn't dream of running a business and just making changes without getting my staff together and saying 'This is what we are going to do together and this is how it will affect you', and then you get people working **with** you; but this anticipation, what appears to be a void in communication, is bad.

(Anticipation refers to the changeover of the responsibility for the school from the Health to the Education Department).

At a meeting of the parent association with the chairman of the Health Committee I asked some pertinent questions: I said, 'If this is such an important meeting why is the local Medical Officer of Health not present?' and the chairman said 'I will answer the questions', and I rather took the line, 'Well I would like my questions answered by an expert' . . . What annoyed me was there was not another parent in the audience who got up and said 'Will you please answer the question Mr Davis has put?' I was absolutely on my own, so I shut up, because once I get my teeth into something then I like to see the conclusion. On the other hand, at a meeting like that with limited time, and they jolly well see it's limited time to answer questions, you don't like to hog the meeting because the rest of the audience will just react against you, but I would like to know what we are supposed to accomplish; it seems to be a dead end every time, you get so far . . .

Mr Peters also said repeatedly during the interview 'They never tell you anything', 'You have to push all the time', 'They don't understand'. He felt that the authorities view him as a troublemaker and that he may not get what he is entitled to because he is always prepared to speak his mind.

The school is obviously the greatest help the parents receive. What is less satisfactory than the progress the school has achieved with the child, continues to be the quality of communication with the school. This problem must not be seen in isolation. Most schools and institutions do not find it easy to communicate with parents and outsiders. Nor can it be said, in fairness, that there is a complete absence of communication or that we have ever experienced great difficulties with the staff. Letters to the school are answered promptly and with great sympathy. Dates for closing, holidays and any administrative matter come to us on 'banda' sheets and that works well enough.

As we live more than five miles away from the centre there cannot be the easy 'dropping in' that some of our best infant and junior schools encourage. There is the phone, but one doesn't like to bother anyone unless it is an urgent matter, in case the teacher is busy in her room. In any case not all parents have phones and not everyone talks comfortably on them.

There are parent afternoons and evenings: these are semi-formal events when both sides are probably on their 'best behaviour'. They ensure contact with some staff and are therefore to be welcomed; it is doubtful, however, whether staff have time to absorb information. What parents learn from these occasions is not certain. At best, parents will be completely satisfied by the meeting: to them it represents all that is wanted and that is the impression I gained from two of the interviews. The best communication is achieved at our school from class meetings, where the teacher meets the parents in her classroom after lunch or after school hours and general discussion of problems can develop.

Evidence from 'normal' secondary schools suggests that this is not always the case. When parents meet teachers both sides are likely to erect defences; the staff may be anxious: they can easily be much younger than the parents and they may feel less confident in their teaching techniques than they would care to admit to an outsider. Everyone who has taught knows this feeling of not having done enough. Furthermore, with mentally handicapped children progress, though often real, is slow and perhaps less apparent to those in constant contact with the children. Only today, when we went on an outing, did it strike us how much better behaved David was compared with a very similar occasion a year ago. So the teacher may feel that there is nothing to report, or that any indication of progress may be seized on by parents who are hungry for encouragement, which in the end will lead to nothing but disappointment.

As a professional group, teachers do not find it easy to talk to parents, perhaps for the same reasons they do not find it easy to talk to each other about their work. They tend to be cut off from one another in the classroom, and talking 'shop' is not always encouraged in the staffroom. This is particularly true of schools where staff relations are based on a strict hierarchy and junior staff are expected to be seen rather than heard. Asking for advice or discussing problems can be felt to be an admission of failure. One of the lessons many young teachers learn quickly is that it is best to keep oneself to oneself and to let others assume that there are no problems. Fortunately, this does not seem to be the case at our local school.

Parents bring their own difficulties into the situation: the very fact of having a mentally handicapped child is, for them, a failure. Whatever the inner feelings, when we face society most of us put on a brave front and the pain is hidden. The tradition of the stiff upper-lip has its uses in war but I am more doubtful of its value when we are dealing with our children.

The parent—teacher association should be the place where experience and expertise can be shared. The degree of difficulty we experience in bringing up our handicapped children may vary, but the PTA should avoid at all costs setting up a kind of jolly club where there is so much activity that no one can be his true self. There should be a place somewhere where one does not have to pretend that all is well and that all our children need are annual outings and Christmas parties. Normal people, and sometimes even those who have mentally handicapped children, often seem to think the children are 'deprived' and a clear distinction must be made between 'deprived' and 'handicapped'. To other people who do not really understand what it is like to have a

handicapped child we must become bores because we
complain all the time. If the parent—teacher association is a
place where genuine communication can take place, teachers
have something of real value to give. They are more detached,
have some professional expertise and can therefore help
parents with bringing up the child they are both in contact
with. One party **can** bring up the child without constant
consultation with the other, but this seems uneconomical in
experience and even in practical terms.

Consistency and continuity are important factors in all
education and how, for example, can teachers and parents
succeed in toilet-training unless they communicate with one
another on the approach they have to the problem, what
sanctions or encouragement they believe work and what
words they use? We say 'pee' and school says 'toilet' and
the child has to learn two words instead of one. This seems
wasteful when one remembers that the mentally handicapped
child has a limited vocabulary to work with in any case.

In all the work of the school the parents play a peripheral
part and I wish we could change this. Surely a case conference
without a parent present must be an extraordinarily one-sided
affair. I am not claiming that parents should be allowed access
to all information at all times; part of the expertise of the
teacher must be to know what can safely be disclosed and
what must best be concealed. There is rarely agreement on this
point: patients want to be told when they are mortally ill; the
majority of doctors think they would be better off without
this knowledge. If the school had a clear idea of the parents'
maturity and capacity to cope with information they would
surely allow them greater participation? One of the problems in
our society that we must learn to solve is the involvement of
all in the running of the community to a greater extent than
seems possible at the moment. In all our institutions we who
pay for them through our taxes and rates, who send our
children to them, are completely excluded from the processes of
consultation. With far too many of us, non-consultation has
become a way of life, to the extent that it is neither expected
nor demanded any more. Those of us who do want to
participate are branded either as idealists or troublemakers.

One of the main concerns of parents is how far their child will be able to work with other people in later life

It seems to us, and to some of the parents we discussed the problem with, that the moment one has a misfortune one becomes exposed to 'having things done for one'. This helps at first, but in the long run it deprives one of the will to participate or to make constructive suggestions. In several of the parents and in ourselves I have noticed a kind of exhaustion that comes from having to deal with children who make excessive demands. If the authorities that help us to bring up our children value what we can contribute, they should seriously consider bringing in the parents as much as they can and on as many levels of decision-making as possible. Of course there will be apathy and possibly resentment, but it could also be the beginning of a therapeutic process that involves the community and does not leave the individual family unit with a feeling of isolation and hopelessness. (The Joint Advisory Committee for the Mentally Handicapped, recently established in Bristol, may well become a valuable channel for communication.)

Comments and recommendations

1 Parents should be made aware of any benefits they may be entitled to such as the Attendance Allowance.

2 A member of the local authority Social Services Department should visit the family and explain what help they are entitled to. This might be done in the form of a check-list.

3 Clear information should be given to parents well before the child's fifth birthday as to what education he or she will receive if the child is not already attending a training school or special unit. It should not be left to the parents to try and ascertain this information for themselves. Every child has the right to some form of education from the age of five onwards.

4 Communication between parents and teachers could often be considerably better. Parents and teachers working with the child, but in isolation from one another, will not help that child to achieve maximum progress. Parents should be encouraged to drop in to the school informally, perhaps to collect the child where this is feasible — and informal meetings between parents and teachers should be arranged regularly. Case conferences should include the parents wherever possible.

5 If the child cannot start at the centre till the age of five, some form of playgroup or nursery class is essential.

6 Some schools have started a diary for each child which passes between school and home. This ensures that teaching is not being duplicated and that similar methods are used.

CHAPTER 9 **THE FUTURE**

None of the children of the parents interviewed here was more than eight years old and not very much was said about the future, except that they added gloomily that they did not know what would happen when they themselves were dead. The prospect is not a happy one and I share this reluctance to look too far ahead. We manage from day to day the best we can, we fear a crisis when either one of us cannot fully support the other, and therefore old age and incapacity are deeply dreaded. The mentally handicapped child, particularly if he is a mongol, is very likely to outlive his parents. This possibility throws a heavy burden on brothers and sisters.

If the family is very well-off they can perhaps make provision in a private home, but for the majority there is the prospect of hospital for the mentally handicapped. These places have not had a good press recently and the publication of the Committee of Inquiry into the Whittingham and Ely hospitals only confirms the fears that, as a parent, one already has. Like so many of our other institutions they still have structures that may have been adequate in another century but fail to meet the needs of present-day society. It is no use just making scapegoats of some overworked and underpaid nurses and hospital administrators and hoping that improvement will come because of some punitive measures. However even if money is spent on a monumental scale it will be a long time before these institutions will approximate to a reasonably good home.

The mentally handicapped do not make a very powerful political lobby: they do not fill the postbag of their MPs with mail, and I fear that it is quite likely that more dramatic and well-organized claims will take priority and will attract both funds and votes. If institutions are seen to be inadequate families will hold on to the child as long as they can and probably longer, and so all the difficulties described here will continue and the family will not receive all the support it needs.

Home farms and hostels exist, of course, but they will only cater for a few and at this stage we cannot be sure that our David will be up to the educational standard that home farms, for example, quite reasonably demand. Hostels are still in the experimental stage and a great deal of public prejudice will have to be overcome before they can be opened in sufficient numbers. There have been distressing instances when the neighbourhood has refused to allow hostels to be opened. There seems to be fear that property values will diminish, and that mentally handicapped adults will be a threat to young children, young women and widows.

Mentally handicapped children still may have something lovable about them; they may be cuddly and their very helplessness appeals. Mentally handicapped adults are a different matter. The National Society for Mentally Handicapped Children is treated generously by the public. One fears that mentally handicapped adults, if they were presented to the public realistically, would not do so well. Their potential strength and sexuality are threats, there is the popular stereotype of the 'sex maniac' and evidently there is widespread fear and rejection.

Again there is some progress: the campaigns of MIND (the National Association for Mental Health) have made some impact, the mass media are sympathetic to the mentally handicapped and there have been sensitive and intelligent films. Schoolchildren and students are making conscious efforts to contact adults in institutions and the mystery and dread may be diminishing. Nevertheless there are reactions to hostels in the community and they indicate the depth of feeling about mentally handicapped adults.

Sometimes when I am depressed I think that I have done my duty by the child and when I am old and incapacitated it will be the turn of the community which sets such a great store on the preservation of life and insists that we look after our mentally handicapped child. When David was born I joined an insurance scheme: for about twelve pounds annually (income-tax deductible) there would be someone who took an interest in David, sent him birthday cards, Christmas cards and presents and looked after his interests in general. Immediately after the birth I was desperate to do something positive and was somehow so appalled by the immediate present that I projected my anxieties into the distant future. When the other two boys, Simon and Toby, were born I came to think that this was not money well spent, and cancelled the policy. The insurance company generously released me from the contract to pay twelve pounds annually for the rest of my life.

The mentally handicapped adult will have to be accepted by the community as a whole and the problem his very existence creates will have to be faced. He is not a danger but he needs care and supervision, education and a social life. If he is just locked up in an institution he will become an institutionalized cabbage and the bit of personality he has built up during the years and the education at the training centre will just be lost.

The longer he stays at home the greater the burden on the family. It is not just a question of parents but brothers and sisters; they have their own lives to lead and have the right to establish families of their own. We must take great care that having lived with mental handicap they will not lose the confidence to start a family of their own or that because of guilt feelings and anxieties they will not realize their own full human potential.

Comments and recommendations

1 There are fears about how the parents will cope in old age and not much is said about this at present. As the mentally handicapped live longer these fears must be taken into account by those who come into contact with the parents.

2 State and local authority residential provisions need a great deal of moral and financial support. They must be seen to be good and adequate so that parents will send their children to them with greater confidence. If this confidence is lacking they will hold on to the handicapped adult longer than they should and the burden on the family as a whole will not be relieved.

3 Small units and hostels that are part of the community seem to be the best answer, but if they are to be established in adequate numbers there will have to be a great deal of educational and public-relations work, backed by authorities who are convinced that this is the right thing to do.

4 The mentally handicapped have normal sexual needs but these are frightening to the public at large. It is no use pretending that this need does not exist, or pretending that the adults are just children. We must face the implication of these needs rather than rationalize these fears into anxieties that property values might decrease, and a belief that the mentally handicapped should be locked up in institutions away from all contact with the community.

Further information

Publications

These are books which have helped me in my own understanding of the problem or which have given some supporting evidence to more general statements I have made.

D. Bull, **Family Poverty,** Duckworth, 1967.

E. Cooper and R. Henderson, **Something Wrong?,** Arrow Books, 1974.

J. W. B. Douglas, **The Home and the School,** MacGibbon & Kee, 1964.

B. Furneaux, **The Special Child,** Penguin, 1973.
This ranges over the whole field of special education and is written with some authority and sympathy. There is a good bibliography for anyone who wants to look into the problems more deeply.

E. Goffman, **Stigma,** Penguin, 1968.
Traces the idea of a 'spoilt identity' and the defences those with a spoilt identity put up against outsiders.

D. Hooper and J. Roberts, **Disordered Lives,** Longman, 1967.
A useful introduction to families under stress. New edition (1973) by the National Marriage Guidance Council.

J. and E. Newson, **Patterns of Infant Care,** Penguin, 1965, and **Four Years Old in an Urban Community,** Penguin, 1970.
Two useful books on the changing patterns of child-rearing.

J. Parfit, **Services for the Young Handicapped Child,** National Children's Bureau, 1972.
This book gives an overview of provisions made in various parts of the country. It may be a source of ideas for parents wanting to suggest projects to their local authority.

B. Shepperdson, 'Attending to Need', **New Society,** vol. 24.
Describes a study of thirty-seven families with mongol
children and asks whether all those who need it get the
Attendance Allowance.

A. Stoller and R. D. Collman, 'Incidence of infective hepatitis
followed by Down's Syndrome nine months later', **Lancet,**
vol. 2, 1969, p. 1221.

J. Stone and F. Taylor, **Handbook for Parents with a
Handicapped Child,** Home and School Council, 1972.
Packed with useful addresses and information with emphasis on
the inclusion of parents in decision-making. It is available
from CASE Publications, 17 Jacksons Lane, Billericay, Essex.

P. Wilmott, **Family and Kinship in East London,** Penguin,
1957.
A useful book which describes much of the breakdown in old
family structures and the consequent lessening of support from
within the family.

One to One, 'Kith and Kids', obtainable from Maurice Collins,
58 The Avenue, London N10.
A report about a project of working with handicapped children
on a one-to-one basis of child and volunteer.

Parents Information Bulletin No. 13, Mental Handicap A—Z,
NSMHC.
Your questions answered — it gives the addresses of Regional
Welfare Secretaries and supplies practical answers to the questions
most often asked by parents. It will be invaluable to people
working with the mentally handicapped and their families.

Other useful publications are obtainable from NSMHC
Bookshop, 86 Newman Street, London W1P 4AR:

P. Brinkworth and J. Collins, **Improving Your Mongol Baby,**
NSMHC.

A. D. B. and A. M. Clarke, **Practical Help for Parents of
Retarded Children,** Hull Society for Mentally Handicapped
Children, 1969.

L. Dittman, **The Mentally Handicapped Child at Home,** NSMHC.

C. Jackson, **They Say My Child's Backward,** NSMHC.

K. Solly, **The Different Boy,** NSMHC.

The Child with Mongolism, NSMHC.

Your Mongol Baby, MIND (The National Association for Mental Health), 22 Harley Street, London W1N 2ED.

Organizations

Concord Films Council Ltd, Nacton, Ipswich, Suffolk IP10 0JZ are a non-profit-making body and are the best source of films about mental handicap.

A catalogue for clothing for the handicapped and disabled is published by the King's Fund Centre, 24 Nutford Place, London W1. Ideas for toys for handicapped children may be obtained from Medical Recording Service Foundation, Kitts Croft Writtle, Chelmsford CM1 3EH.

For genetic counselling, write to The Social Services Department, MIND (The National Association for Mental Health), 22 Harley Street, London W1N 2ED.

For information on birth control, ring the Brook Advisory Clinic, 01-580-2991, or the Family Planning Association, 01-636-7866.

Illustration acknowledgements

Page 12 to Peter Brandt; pages 38, 42—3, 54, 59, 62—3, 74—5, 82—3, 90, 100—101 to Robert Vente; page 66 to Charles Hannam; pages 97, 115 to Susan Beihoffer; pages 108—9 to Chris Steele-Perkins; page 114 to Martin Weaner; page 118 to Mark Edwards; page 119 to Janine Wiedel.

Index